CONVERSAT...
WITH SCRIPTURE:

THE PARABLES

WILLIAM BROSEND

For Dottie
Blessings

MOREHOUSE PUBLISHING
HARRISBURG NEW YORK

Morehouse Publishing and the Anglican Association of Biblical Scholars thank the Louisville Institute for their interest in and support of this series.

Morehouse Publishing, P.O. Box 1321, Harrisburg, PA 17105

Morehouse Publishing is an imprint of Church Publishing Incorporated.

Cover art: *The Good Shepherd*. All rights reserved Vie de Jésus MAFA, 24 rue du Maréchal Joffre, F-78000 VERSAILLES, www.jesusmafa.com. Vie de Jesus Mafa (Life of Jesus Mafa) is a coherent set of pictures illustrating 61 scenes of the New Testament. They are published in different size posters (10x15 to 70x100 cm) and on videotape. They have been shared with the world for more than 25 years with ongoing success, especially where people have a special feeling for a black Jesus in African surroundings. Jesus brought to life again speaks to each of us with one's own language and culture. He's become one of us.

Cover design: Laurie Klein Westhafer

Series design by Beth Oberholtzer

Library of Congress Cataloging-in-Publication Data

Brosend, William F. (William Frank), 1954–
    Conversations with Scripture : the parables / William Brosend.
        p.   cm.
    Includes bibliographical references (p.   ).
    ISBN-13: 978-0-8192-2167-4 (pbk.)
    1. Jesus Christ—Parables.   I. Title.
BT375.3.B76   2006
226.8'06—dc22

2006027957

Printed in the United States of America

06 07 08 09 10 11   10 9 8 7 6 5 4 3 2 1

Conversations with Scripture: The Parables
is dedicated to
John R. Donohue, S.J.
who opened my ears to hear

With many such parables he spoke the word to them, as they were able to hear it; he did not speak to them except in parables. (Mark 4:33–34a)

Gracious Lord, we praise You and bless You for coming to us in ways that we are able to see and to hear: in Your child Jesus, and in His blessed words, most chiefly in parable. Grant that we will be ever aware of all the ways that You speak to us, and use us, we pray, to show and share the glorious good news that Jesus Christ is Lord, to Your glory, now and forever.

AMEN.

I will open my mouth in a parable; I will utter dark sayings from of old, things that we have heard and known, that our ancestors have told us. We will not hide them from their children; we will tell to the coming generation the glorious deeds of the LORD. (Psalm 78:2–4)

Almighty God, who calls to your people by your holy and blessed Word, open our hearts to hear your Word for us, and so inspire us by your Holy Spirit that our lives may show forth your living Word in all that we say and we do, to the glory of your Word made flesh, even Jesus Christ your Son our Lord, who with you and the Holy Spirit lives and reigns, now and forever.

AMEN.

CONTENTS

INTRODUCTION
TO THE SERIES

To talk about a distinctively Anglican approach to Scripture is a daunting task. Within any one part of the larger church that we call the Anglican Communion there is, on historical grounds alone, an enormous variety. But as the global character of the church becomes apparent in ever-newer ways, the task of accounting for that variety, while naming the characteristics of a distinctive approach, becomes increasingly difficult.

In addition, the examination of Scripture is not confined to formal studies of the kind addressed in this series of parish studies written by formally trained biblical scholars. Systematic theologian David Ford, who participated in the Lambeth Conference of 1998, rightly noted that although "most of us have studied the Bible over many years" and "are aware of various academic approaches to it," we have "also lived in it" and "inhabited it, through worship, preaching, teaching and meditation." As such, Ford observes, "The Bible in the Church is like a city we have lived in for a long time." We may not be able to account for the history of every building or the architecture on every street, but we know our way around and it is a source of life to each of us.[1]

That said, we have not done as much as we should in acquainting the inhabitants of that famed city with the architecture that lies within. So, as risky as it may seem, it is important to set out an introduction to the highlights of that city—which this series proposes to explore at length. Perhaps the best way in which to broach that task is to provide a handful of descriptors.

The first of those descriptors that leaps to mind is familiar, basic, and forever debated: *authoritative*. Years ago I was asked by a colleague who belonged to the Evangelical Free Church why someone with as much obvious interest in the Bible would be an Episcopal priest. I responded, "Because we read the whole of Scripture and not just the parts of it that suit us." Scripture has been and continues to play a singular role in the life of the Anglican Communion, but it has rarely been used in the sharply prescriptive fashion that has characterized some traditions.

Some have characterized this approach as an attempt to navigate a via media between overbearing control and an absence of accountability.[2] But I think it is far more helpful to describe the tensions not as a matter of steering a course between two different and competing priorities, but as the complex dance necessary to live under a very different, but typically Anglican notion of authority itself. *Authority*, you see, shares the same root as the word "to author" and as such, refers first and foremost, not to the *power* to *control* with all that both of those words suggest, but to the capacity to *author creativity*, with all that both of those words suggest. As such, the function of Scripture is to carve out a creative space in which the work of the Holy Spirit can yield the very kind of fruit associated with its work in the Church. The difficulty, of course, is that for that space to be creative, it is also necessary for it to have boundaries, much like the boundaries we establish for other kinds of genuinely creative freedom—the practice of scales for concert pianists, the discipline of work at the bar that frees the ballerina, or the guidance that parents provide for their children. Defined in this way, it is possible to see the boundaries around that creative space as barriers to be eliminated, or as walls that provide protection, but they are neither.

And so the struggle continues with the authority of Scripture. From time to time in the Anglican Communion, it has been and will be treated as the raw material of buttresses that protect us from the complexity of navigating without error the world in which we live. At other times, it will be treated as the ancient remains of a city to be cleared away in favor of a brave new world. But both approaches are rooted, not in the limitations of Scripture, but in our failure to welcome the creative space we have been given.

For that reason, at their best, Anglican approaches to Scripture are also *illuminative*. William Sloan Coffin once observed that the problem with Americans and the Bible is that we read it like a drunk uses a lamppost. We lean on it, we don't use it for illumination. Leaning on Scripture—or having the lamppost taken out completely— are simply two very closely related ways of failing to acknowledge the creative space provided by Scripture. But once the creative space is recognized for what it is, then the importance of reading Scripture illuminatively becomes apparent. Application of the insight Scripture provides into who we are and what we might become is not something that can be prescribed or mapped out in detail. It is only a conversation with Scripture, marked by humility, that can begin to spell out the particulars. Reading Scripture is, then, in the Anglican tradition a delicate and demanding task, that involves both the careful listening for the voice of God and courageous conversation with the world around us.

It is, for that reason, an approach that is also marked by *critical engagement* with the text itself. It is no accident that from 1860 to 1900 the three best-known names in the world of biblical scholarship were Anglican priests, two of whom were Bishops: B. F. Westcott, J. B. Lightfoot, and F. J. A. Hort. Together the three made contributions to both the church and the critical study of the biblical text that became a defining characteristic of Anglican life.

Of the three, Westcott's contribution, perhaps, best captures the balance. Not only did his work contribute to a critical text of the Greek Testament that would eventually serve as the basis for the English Revised Version, but as Bishop of Durham he also convened a conference of Christians to discuss the arms race in Europe, founded the Christian Social Union, and mediated the Durham coal strike of 1892.

The English roots of the tradition are not the only, or even the defining characteristic of Anglican approaches to Scripture. The church, no less than the rest of the world, has been forever changed by the process of globalization, which has yielded a rich *diversity* that complements the traditions once identified with the church.

Scripture in Uganda, for example, has been read with an emphasis on private, allegorical, and revivalist applications. The result has been a tradition in large parts of East Africa which stresses the reading of Scripture on one's own; the direct application made to the contemporary situation without reference to the setting of the original text; and the combination of personal testimony with the power of public exhortation.

At the same time, however, globalization has brought that tradition into conversation with people from other parts of the Anglican Communion as the church in Uganda has sought to bring the biblical text to bear on its efforts to address the issues of justice, poverty, war, disease, food shortage, and education. In such a dynamic environment, the only thing that one can say with certainty is that neither the Anglican Communion, nor the churches of East Africa, will ever be the same again.

Authoritative, illuminative, critical, and varied—these are not the labels that one uses to carve out an approach to Scripture that can be predicted with any kind of certainty. Indeed, if the word *dynamic*— just used—is added to the list, perhaps all that one can predict is still more change! And, for that reason, there will be observers who (not without reason) will argue that the single common denominator in this series is that each of the authors also happens to be an Anglican. (There might even be a few who will dispute that!)

But such is the nature of life in any city, including one shaped by the Bible. We influence the shape of its life, but we are also shaped and nurtured by it. And if that city is of God's making, then to force our own design on the streets and buildings around us is to disregard the design that the chief architect has in mind.

—Frederick W. Schmidt
Series Editor

AUTOBIOGRAPHICAL
NOTE

A long, long time ago, in my Baptist days, I came to Vanderbilt Divinity School intending to pursue a Master of Divinity degree, followed by a Ph.D. in Old Testament. I came to Vanderbilt because of the influence of Timothy Sedgwick, now professor of theological ethics at the Virginia Theological Seminary, who not only introduced me to Vanderbilt, but also to Anglicanism.

God (surprise!) had other plans. God introduced me to John Donahue, a Jesuit priest and New Testament scholar who, first in a course on the Gospel of Mark and then in a legendary course on the parables of Jesus, so thoroughly changed my plan of studies that I did my doctorate in *New* Testament at the University of Chicago, Father Donahue's alma mater, and wrote my dissertation on parable (and allegory) in the Gospel of Mark. So other than changing fields and changing communions, life went pretty much as I expected when I first arrived in Nashville.

Now, wonder of wonders, I am back in Tennessee, teaching homiletics at the School of Theology at the University of the South in Sewanee, one of our eleven Episcopal seminaries. After more than twenty years as an American Baptist pastor and teacher, I am an Episcopal priest privileged to help shape a new generation of clergy for the Church. Oddly and circuitously, I am doing exactly what I thought I would be doing so many years ago. You have to love a God with such a great sense of humor.

The parables of Jesus are important to me for many reasons, most of which will be obvious by the time you finish this book, so only a few need be noted here. First, the parables were Jesus' favorite way to preach and teach, and as someone who preaches and teaches *about* Jesus I believe content and form are both important. Better understanding *how* Jesus taught will help us better understand *what* he taught. Second, I have found that the Gospel of Mark is correct in saying that parables are the way the people of God best hear the Word of God (4:33–34). In a variety of settings, from seminary to Sunday school, classes on the parables of Jesus are consistently appealing. Finally, as I explain in the last chapter, I also believe that learning how to interpret the parables helps us in our interpretation of the whole of Scripture. So the work we do together on the parables may help you be a better student of the Bible in unexpected ways.

I have been preparing most of my life to write this little volume on the parables, and I have to admit that I had a marvelous time doing so. I pray that you will be informed and formed by it, and hope that you will enjoy it a bit in the process.

Blessings!

Bill Brosend
Feast of St. Francis of Assisi, 2006
Sewanee, Tennessee

INTRODUCTION

The great preacher and teacher of preaching, Fred B. Craddock, showed us long ago in *As One without Authority* and *Overhearing the Gospel*[1] that the surest way to put an audience to sleep is to "tell 'em what you're gonna tell 'em, tell 'em, and tell 'em what you told them," also known as "three points and a poem." We have come to call Dr. Craddock's method "inductive preaching" and although there are those in the homiletics guild who decry it, you should be very, very glad if your priest believes in it. We could also, I think, call Dr. Craddock's method parabolic preaching, not because the preacher will tell you a story nearly as interesting as the stories Jesus told, but because he or she will draw on the same sort of creativity and exploration that Jesus did—and because the listener will experience the wonderful sense of discovery that Jesus' listeners experienced when they heard the parables live and in person.

Another reason to bring up the preaching analogy is that sermons, like the parables of Jesus, are (or should be) *oral*—meant to be heard, not read. One of the things we are absolutely certain about the historical Jesus is that he was a teacher, and that his preferred mode of teaching was the parable, a form he did not invent but surely perfected. Do yourself a favor as you read this book and every now and then read one of the parables out loud—or better, have someone read it to you. While some of the playfulness and irony found in Greek is lost in English (I happen to think Jesus likely spoke Greek, though he would not have regularly taught in anything other than Aramaic), it is still worth the effort to be ones who have ears to hear (Mark 4:9 and lots of other endings to parables).

I make a ridiculous claim in the pages to follow: learning how to read the parables is key to knowing how to read Scripture. It is because I believe that claim that I wrote this book, and regularly teach classes and courses on parable interpretation. I make the claim not because I am ignorant of the many other literary and rhetorical genres found in both testaments, nor because I think we should apply one interpretive method to the whole of Scripture. In fact, I believe the opposite—attention to genre is important, and each genre deserves its own, appropriate methodolgy. However, there is something about the way we must approach the parables—reverently but rigorously, seriously but not literally, expecting to discover something we did not know, and to be delighted in both the process and product that can be usefully applied to the Psalter, Prophets, Epistles—even Torah and history.

First, though, we need to spend some time in the wonderful school of the parables of Jesus. The first chapter is the dreaded but necessary introduction to studying the parables, with a blessedly brief bit of history and a discussion of the socio-rhetorical method to be applied in the chapters that follow. Chapters two through five organize the parables thematically rather than by source, type, or some other category. To the extent possible, many of the parable texts are included, but it will certainly not hurt you to bring your Bible with you when you read each chapter. Along the way I treat most, but by no means all, of the parables. I hope we look at your favorite. Saving the Good Samaritan for the last chapter, I conclude by returning to the idea that learning how to read the parables trains us to read the whole of Scripture.

Somewhere along the way someone convinced me that studying the Bible was fun. Not like watching *The Daily Show* or an old Robin Williams routine, but an occasion when the laughter of self-discovery is more than appropriate. Sometimes, frankly, Jesus is trying to be funny and we just don't get it because, well, we're in church, for heaven's sake. In other words, enjoy!

 I Love to Tell the Story:
Jesus the Storyteller

Once upon a time . . . a long time ago, in a galaxy far, far away . . . there was a man who had two sons. . . .

However they begin, we love stories. At bedtime, at the movieplex, or at the beach, we love a good story. We even like a good story in church. Be honest. The last time you thought to yourself, "That was a good homily," was it because of the incisive exegesis and clear expression of doctrine, or because there were a couple of memorable stories that captured your imagination and vividly related Scripture and doctrine to your life?

No collection—and that is what the Bible is—can match Scripture when it comes to exciting, compelling, and memorable storytelling. From the Garden to the Ark; first Abram, then Joseph, and finally Moses in Egypt; the judges Deborah, Gideon, and Samuel; the kings Saul, David, and Solomon, the "history" of the Hebrew Bible is one powerful story after another. The same is true of the prophets, Elijah and Elisha of course, but also of the great classic, literary prophets like Isaiah, Jeremiah, and Amos, who both told stories (Isa 5) and had wonderful stories told about them (Isa 6).

But wait just a minute. What do I mean by "story"? Is not a "story" a literary fiction, created to "profit with delight" and not to be confused with history (her/his-story), which is a narrative of events recounted by an eyewitness or credible reporter? Yes. And no, at least when it comes to the collection that is for us Holy Scripture. There is a distinction between story and history, but in the Bible it is neither always clear nor finally absolute. Before and after we ask, "Did it happen?" we must ask "What does it mean?" because as people of faith, we are seekers after the truth, and not just the facts.

Before you toss this idea aside as of shaky value and questionable orthodoxy suggested by one more overeducated scholar, consider this: what is the difference between a story that starts "once upon a time" and one that begins "there was a man who had two sons"—that is, between a fairy tale and the story of the Prodigal in Luke 15? Okay, now consider the story of the Prodigal and the "story" of, say, the biblical Jacob, another younger son who ran off to seek fame and fortune in a foreign land? By "story" I mean a narrative, fictional or nonfictional, with a plot that moves from beginning to middle to end. We love stories, from the "story of our nation's history" to the story of Joseph and his brothers to the story of the Good Samaritan.

Jesus, on the evidence of the Synoptic Gospels Matthew, Mark, and Luke, also loved stories—he based his teaching on the stories of his own Hebrew Bible tradition, and he often shared that teaching in the form of a story, a form we usually refer to as "parable." The fourth chapter of the Gospel of Mark offers two conflicting explanations of Jesus' use of parables. The first explanation is found on the lips of Jesus and paralleled in the gospels of Matthew (13:10–17) and Luke (8:9–10), and echoes an important passage in the prophet Isaiah (6:9–10).

Matthew, Mark, and Luke are referred to as the **Synoptic Gospels** because they share the same basic outline, or synopsis, of the events of Jesus' life.

> And he said to them, "To you has been given the secret of the kingdom of God, but for those outside, everything comes in parables; in order that 'they may indeed look, but not perceive, and may indeed listen, but not understand; so that they may not turn again and be forgiven.'" (Mark 4:11–12)

Jesus, it seems, speaks in parables so that no one but the twelve disciples can understand him.

The second explanation, barely twenty verses later, is from the Evangelist himself, and has no parallel in the other canonical gospels (or noncanonical, for that matter).

> With many such parables he spoke the word to them, as they were able to hear it; he did not speak to them except in parables, but he explained everything in private to his disciples. (Mark 4:33–34)

Here it seems that Jesus used parables precisely so that he could be understood by everyone. Except the disciples, who needed individual, if not remedial, tutoring.

Okay, which is it? Did Jesus speak in parables to confuse or to make plain? That question has challenged interpreters for years. On the one hand, many of the parables seem fairly easy to interpret, and it is hard to imagine why Jesus would not want his hearers to understand his message and repent of their sins ("Jesus came to Galilee, proclaiming the good news of God, and saying, 'The time is fulfilled, and the kingdom of God has come near; repent, and believe in the good news'" [Mark 1:14–15]). On the other hand, as we will see, the meaning of more than a few of the parables is anything but obvious, and we must assume that Jesus references Isaiah 6 to connect the difficulty listeners will have with his message to Isaiah's prophecy.

The Christian **"canon"** (Greek for "measuring rod" or standard) refers to the four Gospels and twenty-three other writings we call the New Testament. There are scores of other "gospels" written in the first centuries not up to that standard and hence, **"noncanonical."**

So is there something in the nature of parables themselves that permit both possibilities in a single chapter of the Bible? Yes there is, and at the risk of sending you screaming from the room I will name it—polyvalency. Our conversation with the parables will be founded on an important assumption—that a parable "means" more than one thing, or has multiple (poly) meanings (valency). Such multiplication of meaning can be over time, across cultures, and in different renditions of the same or similar stories. Those multiple meanings can also occur in the same room at the same time looking at the same

Our conversation with the parables will be founded on an important assumption—that a parable "means" more than one thing, or has multiple (poly) meanings (valency).

passage—for example, you might disagree with my emphasis in reading a parable later in this book. A for-instance might help. Jesus told the story of the Pharisee and the tax collector in Luke 18:10–14:

> "Two men went up to the temple to pray, one a Pharisee and the other a tax collector. The Pharisee, standing by himself, was praying thus, 'God, I thank you that I am not like other people: thieves, rogues, adulterers, or even like this tax collector. I fast twice a week; I give a tenth of all my income.' But the tax collector, standing far off, would not even look up to heaven, but was beating his breast and saying, 'God, be merciful to me, a sinner!' I tell you, this man went down to his home justified rather than the other. . . ."

Jesus said "Pharisee" and most of his audience thought of a party of passionately faithful, rigorously obedient, leaders of the faith. We hear "Pharisee" and think "hypocrite"—in no small part because of this parable. But because we hear the word so differently, the parable "works" differently for us than it did for Jesus' audience. Nor do we think the same thing when we hear "tax collector"—you might hear a joke about the Internal Revenue Service, but no one calls IRS agents "traitors" or "exploiters." So which interpretation is correct—the one that reads the parable as a condemnation of hypocrisy or the one that finds Jesus calling contemporary standards of righteousness into question? You will have to skip to chapter four to find my answer; the point for now is that there are at least two defensible readings of the parable, differing across time and understandings of the parable's background. That is polyvalency, and as the history of parable interpretation has developed, it has come to be seen as a possibility to embrace, not a problem to be solved.

The History of Parable Interpretation in Four Easy Steps

A number of books, not to mention doctoral dissertations beyond numbering, recount the history of parable interpretation, but that is my problem, not yours. The interested reader may pursue one of the suggested books at end of the chapter for the details, yet a lot of what we need to know for this study can be summarized in a few paragraphs.

While a precise definition of *parable* is central to the purpose and outline of this study, understood more broadly, parables are part of a

I LOVE TO TELL THE STORY: JESUS THE STORYTELLER

range of literary devices and genres one might group under the rubric "figurative language." In fact, the biblical languages, Hebrew and Greek, stubbornly refused to make neat distinctions between *mashal* (Hebrew) and *parabolē* (Greek) and proverb, allegory, fable, metaphor, simile, and other examples of figurative language found in Scripture. The distinctions found in the history of interpretation, therefore, are taken from the biblical languages, not signaled by them.

Organized simply, one could view the main movements in parable interpretation according to the approach prevailing during each era, and so speak of the allegorical, univocal (or anti-allegorical), historical, and metaphorical periods of interpretation. These periods were of different duration, the allegorical lasting until the latter half of the nineteenth century, the univocal roughly until the 1930s, the historical until the 1960s (though with significant current practitioners and influence), and the metaphorical from the 1970s until today. Not surprisingly, each period is highlighted by one or more dominating figures, whose names will be on the test at the end of this chapter. (All right, there isn't any test, but if there were, those names would be on it, so pay attention.)

ALLEGORICAL INTERPRETATION

Although it is all around us (*Star Wars, The Chronicles of Narnia, The Lord of the Rings*), allegory has been in general disfavor since the Enlightenment, or for at least the last two hundred years. Allegory is a figure of speech or writing that generates meaning by creating a series of analogies, each figure in the allegory representing a truth about the world to which the figure points. But for the previous two millennia allegory, and when it came to the parables of Jesus, allegorical interpretation was all the rage. Most famously with Origen around 200 CE (who was informed by the Jewish philosopher Philo of Alexandria, himself a rough contemporary of Jesus), and on through St. Augustine, the Middle Ages, the Reformation, and beyond, to interpret a parable was to read it allegorically. Not that the interpreter discounted the "plain" meaning, but convinced that Jesus would not bother to tell stories that were about, say, ornery servants or unfruitful fig trees, the

> **Allegory** is a figure of speech or writing that generates meaning by creating a series of analogies.

stories must be "about" something else. This basic notion of analogy is key to all parable interpretation, but allegorical interpretation assumes that the analogies are both plural and linear, so that each detail of the narrative is important to the construction of its meaning. St. Augustine's reading of the Good Samaritan is the most (in)famous example. The "man" who goes down to Jericho is Adam. The "thieves" who beat him are the devil and his minions, and what they "strip" him of is his mortality. And so it goes. The "Samaritan" who stops to help is Jesus, the "inn" where he takes him is the Church, and the innkeeper none other than the Apostle Paul (Augustine, *Quaestiones Evangeliorum* 2.19).[1]

A creative, interesting, and influential reading. Like our neighbors poring over *The DaVinci Code* for clues, the ancients used the parables as grist for the allegorical mill. Fun for all, except the parable itself, which often seemed lost in the interpretive process. From the start, with Origen, there were warnings against excessive interpretation and important examples of restraint. But for most of our era allegorical interpretation of the parables—and for that matter most of Scripture—was rule and norm.

Like our neighbors poring over The DaVinci Code for clues, the ancients used the parables as grist for the allegorical mill.

UNIVOCAL INTERPRETATION

Until the groundbreaking work of a German scholar named Adolf Jülicher, whose 1881 book on the parables of Jesus (*Die Gleichnisreden Jesu*)[2] heralded a repudiation of allegorical interpretation—and of allegory in general—and a period of what I have termed "univocal" readings of the parables. Jülicher's genius was in recognizing parable as a rhetorical form, and reading parables for what they had to say and not for what might be read into them. Not that he was immune to the tendency to do so, but he resisted the temptation effectively by insisting that a true parable had only one point of comparison, and therefore only one point. The interpreter's task was to accurately determine what the one point of the parable was, a task both historical and literary. The problem is that parables are capable of having more than one point, and by casting aside allegorical interpretations of parables, he also cast aside allegory. The

Good Samaritan was read by Jülicher as an "example story." To him, the dynamic of the story was beside the point, which was simply to "go and do the same."

HISTORICAL INTERPRETATION

While his influence remained, Jülicher's insistence on a single point of comparison finally failed to convince, and between the World Wars and in the years after the second, guided by such giants at Rudolf Bultmann, Martin Dibelius, and C. H. Dodd, focus shifted to the historical and social background of the parables, and to determining which parables, and what part of those parables, could most likely be attributed to the "historical Jesus." Joachim Jeremias provides a handy touchstone; his *The Parables of Jesus* is still in print and well worth reading more than fifty years after it first appeared in English in 1954.[3] Jeremias was especially interested in distinguishing Jesus' parable from the additions or changes made by the early church and/or the evangelists. They found a series of ten categories of change agents, from translation into Greek to where each Evangelist chose to set the parable in the gospel—with a long look at category seven, allegorization—to explain the difference between the parables as spoken by Jesus and those now found in the gospels. A parallel, and later interest in the historical, is found in the popular work of Kenneth Bailey,[4] who used his experience as a missionary in Palestine to emphasize the rural and pastoral authenticity of the parables, and in the work of New Testament scholars who looked to the social sciences as a key to understanding the world of the parables. Interpreters in this period were fascinated by the Good Samaritan, seeing the story as evidence of the dangers of travel in antiquity, the conflict between Jews and Samaritans, and between the lawyer and Jesus. The dynamic of the story itself was, once again, often lost.

METAPHORICAL INTERPRETATION

The final, and still current, phase of parable interpretation has its roots in the early 1960s, especially in the work of Amos Wilder and Robert Funk, and expanded by Norman Perrin, Dominic Crossan, Dan Via, John Donahue, and a host of others who studied and wrote in the heyday of parable interpretation, roughly 1965 through 1985.[5]

Whether we consider their work postmodern, posthistorical, or post-toasties, their interest was largely in the parable as literary artifact, and particularly in metaphor as the key to understanding parable. I once wrote an article on this wave of scholarship entitled "The Limits of Metaphor," which serves as caution to those who did not heed the warning of my teacher, John Donahue, S. J., about the danger of thinking that "salvation is by metaphor alone." Taking the warning into account, however, allows the interpreter to appreciate and explore the beauty and power of Jesus' verbal creations, masterpieces of language that generate rich interpretations and—in the best of cases—decisive, transforming responses. The Good Samaritan has not been as popular in this period, in part because the story, while dramatic, is straightforward, and because some of the most interesting dynamics—for example, between Jesus and the lawyer, or between this story and the story of Mary and Martha that follows (Luke 10:38–42)—are outside the "world" of the story, a boundary metaphorical interpreters usually chose not to cross.

The Texture of Texts

In the pages that follow, I will interpret the parables consciously informed by an interpretive methodology that is best shared before going further. Usually referred to as "sociorhetorical criticism," it is an attempt to bring together the best of the historical, social-scientific, and metaphorical approaches already described, with a healthy appreciation of the importance of one's point of view and a consistent focus on the religious nature of the text and the faith commitment of the interpreter. Emory University professor Vernon Robbins is credited with championing this method in a number of books and articles, for our purposes most importantly his "guide to interpretation," *Exploring the Texture of Texts* (1996).[6] Robbins outlines five "textures" found in any and every biblical text sociorhetorical, which are summarized here.

INNER TEXTURE

Robbins refers to inner texture as "getting inside a text." To study inner texture is to explore "features in the language of the text itself"; that is, the rhetorical patterns and strategies the author uses to communicate with the reader. One explores inner texture with nothing but the text, perhaps in more than one translation, and a dictionary or lexicon. To study inner texture is to experience and appreciate the power of the text to create a world, to create meaning, to persuade, dissuade, and cajole, without reference to other texts, textual history, sociohistorical and cultural-anthropological insights, etc. The inner texture of the Good Samaritan is the story Jesus told in Luke 10:30–35, without reference to the lawyer's questions, Palestinian topography, or the like.

INTER-TEXTURE

Inter-texture, explains Robbins is "a text's representation of, reference to, and use of phenomena in the 'world' outside the text being interpreted. In other words, the intertexture of a text is the interaction of the language in the text with 'outside' material and physical 'objects,' historical events, texts, customs, values, roles, institutions, and systems."[7] When we explore inter-texture, the relation of the text under study is first and foremost to other *texts*, and secondarily to the "world" behind the other texts. The inter-texture of the Good Samaritan is wonderful, allowing us to explore and apply what we know from elsewhere in Scripture about priests, Levites, and lawyers, how the lawyer's question sounds a lot like that of "rich young man" in Mark 10:17–22, and what to make of the fact that the word Luke uses to describe the "robbers" (10:30, Gk. *leistai*) is the same word Mark uses to describe those who were crucified with Jesus (Mark 15:27).

SOCIOCULTURAL TEXTURE

Examination of the sociocultural texture of a text immerses the interpreter in the world of the text and the world presupposed and evidenced by the text. In our study of sociocultural texture, we attempt to understand the world that produced the text, what it would mean to live in that world, and how our understanding of what it would mean to live in such a world impacts how we understand what it means to "live" the text in our own world. Much more than a consideration of "everyday life in Bible times," fully exploring a text's sociocultural texture means studying the insights of social-scientific criticism, cultural anthropology, and more.

Sociocultural texture is many layered, helping us understand a world where communal values outweigh individual preferences, where family and village ties truly bind, patriarchy reigns unquestioned, patronage controls the economy, and honor and shame are dominant cultural values. In exploring this texture we ask just how dangerous the road was from Jerusalem to Jericho, whether the priest and Levite had to avoid contact with the injured and possibly dead victim so they would not be rendered "unclean" and so not able to perform their Temple duties, and just what kind of medical care the typical innkeeper could offer.

IDEOLOGICAL TEXTURE

In exploring ideological texture, interpreters "put their cards on the table," for the ideological texture is at least as much about the interpreter as it is about the text. Robbins writes, "The issue is the social, cultural, and individual location and perspective of writers and readers. Ideological analysis of a text, then, is simply an agreement by various people that they will dialogue and disagree with one another with a text as a guest in the conversation."[8] Sounds like fun. This is not to say that the texts under study have no ideological biases. But it is the interpreters' bias, and the ideology implicit in any methodology, that is most under scrutiny in this texture. The ideological texture of the Samaritan story begins with the motivation of the lawyer in asking his questions, continues to the relationship of Jews and Samaritans, and does not conclude until readers imagine themselves being confronted with similar questions, dangers, and challenges on the road.

> In exploring ideological texture interpreters "put their cards on the table," for the ideological texture is at least as much about the interpreter as it is about the text.

SACRED TEXTURE

From time to time in my own seminary studies, when confused in our grasp of Husserlian phenomenology or lost in some corner of structuralist hermeneutics, my classmates and I would ask, "What does this have to do with Jesus?" That's what it means to explore the sacred texture. "People who read the New Testament regularly are interested in finding insights into the nature of the relation between human life and the divine. In other words, these readers are interested in locating the way the text speaks about God or gods, or talks about realms of religious life."[9]

For many people, this is the reason for biblical study in the first place. What does this text tell me about God, about Jesus, about salvation, about the nature of the Christian life? How does my understanding of the other textures of this text inform my faith and practice as a believer, or my search for faith? What will I do differently today because I have grappled with this text? In a way, the sacred texture of the Samaritan begins when we realize that the lawyer is asking *our* question—"what must I do to inherit eternal life" (Luke 10:25)—and we are being addressed in all that follows just as much as he was.

A Working Definition

The introduction to the introduction is complete. Having talked about the importance of story and the variety of ways in which stories are important in Scripture, having said more than was needed or appreciated about the history of parable interpretation, and having summarized the sociorhetorical approach to interpretation you will bump into throughout this book, I can finally tell you what a parable is.

There are as many definitions as there are students of the parables, but one has stood the test of time. Writing more than seventy years ago, the eminent British scholar C. H. Dodd wrote:

At its simplest, a parable is a metaphor or simile, drawn from nature or the common life, arresting the hearer by its vividness or strangeness, and leaving the mind in sufficient doubt about its precise application to tease it into active thought.

> At its simplest, a parable is a metaphor or simile, drawn from nature or the common life, arresting the hearer by its vividness or strangeness, and leaving the mind in sufficient doubt about its precise application to tease it into active thought.[10]

This definition will provide the outline for the rest of this book, and along with Vernon Robbin's sociorhetorical method, make our work easy. For that to happen, however, the definition should be examined more closely. We will do so by dividing the definition into five components, first in this chapter, and from time to time in the five chapters to follow.

A PARABLE IS A METAPHOR OR SIMILE

Parables "work" by making comparison, "casting" (*bolē*) two things "beside" (*para*) each other. There are a number of rhetorical forms that "work" in this way, metaphor and simile being the most familiar, and parable, according to Dodd, being a narrative use of metaphor and simile. If someone says that their date was "on them like an octopus," they have used a simile, a comparison including the word "like" ("as" will also do) and conveying not that the date was with an undersea cephalopod with eight limbs, but that the speaker was pushing the date's hands away throughout the evening. A simple metaphor expressing the same sentiment would be, "My date was an octopus." Not literally, of course, but in the sense that this touchy-feely person seemed to have eight hands.

> Parables "work" by making comparison, "casting" (bolē) two things "beside" (para) each other.

Two simple examples from Matthew's gospel:

- First a simile: "The kingdom of heaven is like yeast that a woman took and mixed in with three measures of flour until all of it was leavened" (Matt 13:33).
- Then a metaphor: "Again I tell you, it is easier for a camel to go through the eye of a needle than for someone who is rich to enter the kingdom of God" (Matt 19:24).

We will come back to these short parables; for now notice that while the implications are complex, the comparisons are simple—the kingdom of heaven is compared to the yeast in the dough, a rich person seeking the kingdom is compared to a camel struggling through a needle's eye. While not all metaphors in the gospels are parables, it is such simple (and sometimes complex) juxtapositions that provide the engine enabling parables to make meaning.

PARABLES ARE DRAWN FROM NATURE OR THE COMMON LIFE

Part two of the definition is obvious and tricky—obvious because things like mustard seeds, fig trees, fathers and sons, wedding banquets, and the like are indeed the stuff of everyday life, tricky because they are not necessarily the stuff of *our* lives, but of those in first-century Palestine. While we farm, fish, travel, build, bake, marry, bury, and party, we do none of these things in the ways Jesus' listeners did, and to assume we do is often to miss the dynamic of the parable, if not its message, altogether. Here is where the work of social-scientific criticism comes into play, helping us understand the culture and practices of Jesus' day so that we better understand the dynamics of the parables and grasp their meaning.

Luke's parable of the Great Supper (Luke 14:16–23) provides a good example. A man plans a dinner party and sends invitations, but when the escorts arrive to bring the invited guests they all make excuses (excuses that seem to come from Torah), and so the host tells his slaves to bring in "the poor, the crippled, the blind, and the lame" (a group found in the prophets). When there is still room at the table, the slaves are ordered to "compel" people off the streets, "so that my house may be filled." However we will understand this parable—and we will look at it in detail in chapter five—here's the question: Is that what you do when a guest comes up with a last-minute excuse to miss your party? Probably not, for many reasons, including the fact that because you have a refrigerator, the food would not go to waste, and more tellingly, you do not know the poor well enough to invite them to your home. But in a Palestinian village everybody knew everybody.

PARABLES ARREST THE HEARER BY VIVIDNESS OR STRANGENESS

The summary of the Great Supper just recounted may have already proved the point—strange things happen in parables, and because of the cultural and historical differences, we need to make sure we are not arrested out of ignorance rather than by the vividness of the parable itself. Recall the Pharisee and Tax Collector (Luke 18:10–14) considered on page 4. As long as we make the equation Pharisee = hypocrite, we miss the vividness. If we use the equation Jesus' hearers used (and the one that the historical record supports), Pharisee = person of great faith, then the fact that tax collector (tax collector = greedy traitor selling out his own people to the oppressors) goes home "justified" is shocking.

Consider Mark 12:1–9, the story of the Wicked Tenants: "A man planted a vineyard, put a fence around it, dug a pit for the wine press, and built a watchtower; then he leased it to tenants and went to another country" (v. 1), all of which sounds to those familiar with the Book of Isaiah like the beginning of that book's fifth chapter. What happens when it is time for the harvest, and the vineyard owner wants his share? The tenants beat, wound, and insult the slaves sent to receive payment, and then kill one. That is vivid and strange, but there is more. The owner decides to give them one more chance, and sends his heir, his "beloved son" (if you think this is starting to sound less like a parable and more like an allegory of Jesus' passion you are not alone; more later), whom they also kill. Greed, brutality, and murder—vivid enough for you?

PARABLES LEAVE THE MIND IN DOUBT
ABOUT THEIR PRECISE APPLICATION

One of the issues in parable interpretation is the extent to which their meaning is unclear. While obviously this varies from parable to parable, Dodd's contention is that for the most part the "precise application" is open to question. I think he is right, and not just because of "polyvalency," the point made earlier that metaphors, and thus parables, often have multiple meanings. For one thing, the Evangelists themselves did not always agree on the meaning of a particular parable.

Matthew and Luke both tell the story of the Lost Sheep—a shepherd has one hundred sheep, one strays, he leaves the ninety-nine to look until he finds the lost one—a simple enough story. Luke places the story in the fifteenth chapter, just before the story of the woman with the lost coin and the man with a lost son (better known as the Prodigal). He prefaces the story with the mention of the Pharisees grumbling, "This fellow (Jesus) welcomes sinners and eats with them" (Luke 15:2), while Matthew places the parable after the admonition to "become like children" and immediately prefaces the story with Jesus saying, "Take care that you do not despise one of these little ones; for, I tell you, in heaven their angels continually see the face of my Father in heaven" (Matt 18:10). So is the parable of the Lost Sheep about welcoming sinners or loving the little children? The first readers of the Gospels were not comfortable with Matthew's and Luke's disagreement, and went so far as to add a verse to Matthew not found in the earliest manuscripts about saving the lost. We can appreciate it as an instance of doubt about the parable's precise application. If you need another example, read Luke 16:1–8, the Dishonest Steward. Nobody knows what that is about! (Although I'll do my best in chapter five.)

PARABLES TEASE THE MIND INTO ACTIVE THOUGHT

At the heart of Professor Dodd's understanding of the parables, and of mine, is the conviction that the parables do not just convey meaning. They generate meaning. Jesus did not tell parables so we could say, "Oh yeah, right. I knew that." Instead, he told parables so we would say, "Of course! I never thought of it that way before." And because of this moment of discovery we see many things—if not all things—differently, and not just the issue at hand. Moreover, we share in the creation of the meaning we discover, bringing our own experiences, insights, and faith into the process of interpretation. That is one reason the parables continue to surprise us, and the reason we rarely read the parables the same way each time we encounter them, such as every three years in the Sunday lectionary. We are in a different place emotionally, spiritually, and maybe even geographically, so we engage the parable in a different way, and new insights result.

To return to the Good Samaritan, Luke 10:30–36, though I have heard and preached dozens of sermons on this parable, no sermon is the same because each time the parable struck the preacher—me or someone else—a little differently. One way of thinking about such difference is to recall the characters in the story—traveler, bandits, priest, Levite, Samaritan, innkeeper—not to mention the lawyer whose questions prompt the story, and Jesus who tells it. What if, rather than casting ourselves in the starring role as the Samaritan, thereby making the question, "Who will I help?" we imagine the view of the accosted traveler and so ask, "From whom will I accept help?" That sermon is called "The View from the Ditch," and it is very different from those sermons that focus on the lawyer and his question, or on the Samaritan, or on the bandits. More on this in the last chapter.

So there it is: "A parable is a metaphor or simile, drawn from nature or the common life, arresting the hearer by its vividness or strangeness, and leaving the mind in sufficient doubt about its precise application to tease it into active thought." We have our definition, we have some examples, and we have a method. Before diving in to the parables of growth in the next chapter, a word of caution about what we will *not* be doing in this study.

First, we will not worry about whether a given story is best termed a parable, or similitude, example story, or allegory—this last one paining me because parable and allegory was the subject of my doctoral dissertation. While the distinctions have been important in the history of scholarship, they are not important in the history of Sunday School, and can be safely set aside, although somewhere along the way you must endure a paragraph or footnote about Jesus and allegory. As far as we are concerned, the stories of Jesus, using metaphor as the engine for the creation of meaning and having beginning, middle, and end, can be treated together without great worry.

Second, while Jeremias and other scholars have gone to great lengths to show the importance of the gospel context for their right interpretation, and to track the various ways the early church and the Evangelists have shaped the words of Jesus into the parable forms we know today, by and large we will not attend to this side of parable scholarship. The search for what Crossan, Scott, and others call the "originating parable" or "parabolic kernel" is not without merit, but it is not our concern. If a New Testament scholar asks you, say we are interested in the canonical form of the parables as reflected in 1,900 years of church tradition.

Continuing the Conversation

Those interested in the history of parable interpretation may want to start with Joachim Jeremias' *The Parables of Jesus*, still in print in the second edition (New York: Prentice Hall, 1972). Dodd's classic *The Kingdom in Parables* is no longer available, though you may find it in your parish library or on a used-book website. A complete bibliography covering the first three historical phases of interpretation may be found in Warren S. Kissinger, *The Parable of Jesus: A History of Interpretation and Bibliography*, ATLA Bibliography Series 4 (Methuen, NJ: Scarecrow Press, 1979). For the fourth phase see John R. Donahue, S.J., *The Gospel in Parables* (Philadelphia: Fortress Press, 1988).

I noted that the years from 1965 to 1985 could rightly be considered the most important period in modern parable interpretation. This was no accident, as a seminar on the parables was one of the most dynamic groups in the Society of Biblical Literature at that time. Interestingly, very little publishing of note has been offered on the parables in the last ten to fifteen years, and many titles have fallen out of print. Three should be mentioned, however. Bernard Brandon Scott's *Hear Then the Parable* (Minneapolis: Fortress Press, 1989) remains the most comprehensive recent book on the parables. Arnold Hultgren's *The Parables of Jesus* (Grand Rapids: Eerdmans, 2000) is more recent, and very good, but lacks Scott's extensive introduction. Coming from a particular, and controversial point of view, is William R. Herzog's *Parables as Subversive Speech* (Louisville, KY: Westminster/John Knox Press, 1994).

CHAPTER TWO

We Plow the Fields and Scatter: Parables of Growth

First Grade. It was probably March, and in an age before styrofoam, we cut the tops off our half-pint milk cartons and taped green construction paper around them. With a tablespoon from the teacher, we filled our cartons with dirt, carefully placed two seeds inside (just in case), wrote our name on a popsicle stick that we stuck in the dirt, poured on too much water, and set the carton on the windowsill beside the others. Then we waited, and if we resisted the temptation to continue pouring too much water, by Mother's Day we had our present—miracle of miracles, out of dirt, seed, sun, and water, a plant had grown.

Parables of growth are the most accessible of all Jesus' parables, not just because they are "drawn from nature or the common life," but because they make the most straightforward comparison, offering a metaphor most easily grasped. The ancient teachers of rhetoric recognized this, always including exercises drawing comparisons from the lesser to the greater in their handbooks, and encouraging students to use these comparisons in their speeches.[1] By my count Jesus offered five parables whose central metaphor is about growth: the Sower (Mark 4:3–9; Matt

13:1–9; Luke 8:4–8), the Seed Growing Automatically (Mark 4:26–29), the Mustard Seed (Mark 4:30–32; Matt 13:31–32; Luke 13:18-19), the Wheat and Weeds (Matt 13:24–30), the Unfruitful Fig Tree (Luke 13:6–9); along with others in which growth plays an important role, such as the Wicked Tenants (Mark 12:1–11; Matt 21:33–44; Luke 20:9–18) and the Rich Fool (Luke 12:16–21).

Why all this growth? Of course Jesus and his audience lived in an agricultural society, so the most ready-to-hand analogies were from field and farm. Join that with the simple and accessible nature of the comparison from lesser to greater, and the ways in which a relatively straightforward metaphor like growth can be used in multiple ways, and you have a comparative field ripe for harvest (sorry).

This is not to say that I adhere to the school of parable interpretation that persistently imagines Jesus creating his parables out of what he happened to see and experience on the day when the parable was fashioned. It was the stock of experience, not the day's experience, on which he drew. The setting for Mark 4, in which we find three of the growth parables to be considered in this chapter, was "beside the sea" (Mark 4:1), not in the field. The Wicked Tenants (Mark 12) was told in the Temple precincts, not in a vineyard. Just as your favorite preacher is able to carry you around the world without ever leaving the pulpit, Jesus carried his world with him wherever he stood, or sat, to teach.

Parables and the Kingdom

Of the five parables we'll consider in this chapter, three begin by specifically claiming that the story will tell us something about the kingdom of God, or kingdom of heaven. Indeed the majority of Jesus' parables begin with a phrase something like that which prefaces the parable of the Mustard Seed, "With what can we compare the kingdom of God? What parable shall we use?" (Mark 4:30).

This introduces two problems. First is the matter of context. Was it Jesus, or the Evangelists, who consistently cast the parables as being in some way "about" the kingdom? Second, and most important, is the fact that "kingdom of God/heaven" is hardly itself a static or fixed expression, and so the reader/hearer is left unsure what the point of comparison is comparing itself to. When, to use the example from chapter one, we hear, "My date was an octopus," we know both the person about whom the comparison is being made (the date) and the point of comparison (an octopus).[2] The metaphor arises in the juxtaposition. But when Jesus says, "The kingdom of God is like . . ." even when we "get" the point of comparison (for example, a mustard seed) and appreciate the metaphor that arises from juxtaposing a mustard seed to some other reality (kingdom), we are unsure of the comparison because we have no fixed image of "kingdom of God." In a way it is like being given an equation to solve with two independent variables. $X + Y = 12$ is easy when we are told the value of either X or Y, but when we are not given the value of either X or Y, we are in trouble. The solution, if you will, is to gather up the evidence from all the parables and sayings about the kingdom, and test out our hypotheses of the kingdom on an individual parable after we have come to a tentative conclusion from the entire body of sayings. That is a task for the end of the chapter. In the meantime, we will begin our exploration with the shortest and simplest parable of growth—the mustard seed.

The Parable of the Mustard Seed: One Evangelist's Bush Is Another's Tree.

The parable of the Mustard Seed is found in all three Synoptic Gospels, and in the noncanonical *Gospel of Thomas*.[3] With one major and a few minor variations, the versions are substantially the same.

> He also said, "With what can we compare the kingdom of God, or what parable will we use for it? It is like a mustard seed, which, when sown upon the ground, is the smallest of all the seeds on earth; yet when it is sown it grows up and becomes the greatest of all shrubs, and puts forth large branches, so that the birds of the air can make nests in its shade." (Mark 4:30–32)

Even straightforward parables like this one are not without problems. The first one has to do with a change made by Matthew and Luke from the parable as found in Mark.[4] In Mark, the mustard seed grows to become a "shrub." But in Matthew the seed "becomes the greatest of shrubs and becomes a tree" (13:32), while in Luke "it grew and became a tree" (13:19). Moreover, while all three gospels refer to the mustard seed as "sown," in Mark it is sown on the "earth," in Matthew in a "field," and in Luke in a "garden." The problem? Who "sows" mustard seed? The stuff is like kudzu, or perhaps more closely, like mint—it grows all over the place, whether you want it to or not, creeps into every nook and cranny, and is harder than ivy to kill. The rabbis even forbade it to be planted.[5]

The best explanation for these problems begins with Mark, moves into the verbal preferences of Matthew and Luke, and concludes with a likely attempt to make Mark "better," something the other two do all the time. Mark is responsible for the "sowing"—it is a term he uses repeatedly in his fourth chapter, and naturally uses it here, just as he uses "earth" here and in earlier Sower and Seed Growing Automatically parables. Matthew and Luke use Mark's "sow," but have their own preferences—field and garden—for where the sowing took place. As for the results? Well, come on—what kind of big finish do you get out of a shrub?

Nobody talks about the "majestic boxwood" or the "towering hydrangea." Oaks are majestic and cedars tower. If your comparison is from the lesser to the greater, you want the seed to be the smallest and the result to be the greatest, so the two-foot-tall mustard plant becomes a huge tree, with large branches (Mark has them on his shrub), big enough for bird nests.

Jesus, on the other hand, was likely content with a simple comparison of a tiny seed and a full-grown plant, but placed the emphasis on the small seed (Mark and Matthew have *mikroteron*). What we are to notice is not that the kingdom is great (a tree, not a shrub, for heaven's sake), but that the beginnings are as small as they can be. As we begin to imagine what the kingdom of God/heaven is like, our first lesson from the parables is a simple one. The kingdom of God starts so small you can hardly see it, but when it comes into its own, it is everywhere. You can't miss it.

THE SEED GROWING SECRETLY:
I DON'T KNOW HOW IT HAPPENED BUT IT SURE TASTES GOOD.

The worst grade I received in college was in botany, either a reflection of how tired I was of plant life after years of earning spending money cutting grass with the family push mower, or an anticipation of what a lousy gardener I turned out to be (oddly enough, I do grow a nice lawn, but that's it—just grass). In any case, for all my years of

> Who "sows" mustard seed? The stuff is like kudzu, or perhaps more closely, like mint—it grows all over the place, whether you want it to or not, creeps into every nook and cranny, and is harder than ivy to kill. The rabbis even forbade it to be planted.

formal education, I am as clueless as the farmer in the following parable, found only in Mark and usually known as the "seed growing secretly" in scholarship. The key word in Greek, however, is not "secret" but *automaton*, so I prefer something like The Automatic Seed—something I could use in my garden, come to think of it.

> He also said, "The kingdom of God is as if someone would scatter seed on the ground, and would sleep and rise night and day, and the seed would sprout and grow, he does not know how. The earth produces of itself, first the stalk, then the head, then the full grain in the head.[6] But when the grain is ripe, at once he goes in with his sickle, because the harvest has come." (Mark 4:26–29)

Once again the kingdom of God is compared to a growth process that begins with someone sowing (the Greek word is the same here and in the parable of the Mustard Seed, although the New Revised Standard Version [NRSV] translates it here as "scatter"). It is important to stop and remind ourselves that the metaphor is not the point of comparison, as if we have a simple equation, kingdom = seed. Instead the metaphor arises out of the comparative process, that is, the kingdom = all the words that follow the phrase "as if." There is something about seed sown, the sower sleeping and rising, and the seed sprouting, growing, and bearing fruit without any help from the sower—who at the right time becomes the harvester—that discloses the nature of the kingdom of God.

*The **New Revised Standard Version** (NRSV) is an excellent English translation based on the best available ancient manuscripts of the Bible.*

We also need to take caution, in a way that anticipates a distinction between parable and allegory that we'll develop when we look at the Sower, not to mistake the recitation of the details of growth for an invitation to allegorize (as in Augustine's treatment of the details of the Samaritan's care of the wounded traveler discussed in the chapter one). There is one central comparison—the automatically growing seed—not a series of comparisons such as we will find in the Sower, and that is the difference between parable and allegory. Parable makes meaning out of one central comparison (however many details) while allegory makes meaning through a series of comparisons.

Parable makes meaning out of one central comparison (however many details) while allegory makes meaning through a series of comparisons.

So what do we have here—a stupid farmer who does not understand the process of photosynthesis? Or have we concentrated on the words "he does not know how" when we really should be looking at the word "automatically"? I've tipped my hand on the answer already, but it is worth noting that the lack of "knowing" does not point to the superior wisdom of modern science. Even when we understand the photo-chemical processes that make it possible for edible food to emerge from bare earth, seed, water, and sun, it is no less amazing—and more amazing still when we realize that a little manure makes the end product taste so much better. And even when we "know" we cannot "do," as the taste of a "hothouse tomato" proves every time.

My late Greek teacher, David Wilmot, would chastise me if I did not mention the peculiar choice of vocabulary in this parable. The sower is *anthrōpos*, human being, and the words for sleep and rise, *katheudē* and *egeirētai*, are the words New Testament authors use to describe death and resurrection (most famously at Ephesians 5:14, "Sleepers, awake!"). While the charged terminology invites allegory, it also forces us to deal with the eternal significance of talking about the kingdom of God—while the "seed" is growing, human beings are dying and rising to new life. And just in case we found a way to keep things uncomplicated, we have to deal with a harvest—and that always means judgment.

Our story, then, "works" on multiple levels. At its most basic it is about farming—we can scatter the seed, but we cannot make it grow—that's as true of my garden as it is of the kingdom of God. Lest we confine the meaning of this parable to the span of our earthly life, the parable uses loaded words for sleeping and waking—words used elsewhere in the New Testament for dying and rising—hinting that the kingdom should not be limited by a single lifespan. And then the story moves into the world of the end times, which comes to mind whenever the harvest is in view. But this is not a negative, scary sort of harvest. No trampling of the vineyards where the grapes of wrath are stored (Joel 3:13 and, of course, "The Battle Hymn of the Republic"). This is harvest as fulfillment: the sower planted, waited, and enjoyed a harvest.

What is this adding to our store of knowledge about the kingdom? The parable tells us that the kingdom of God is not up to us—

it grows "of itself," automatically. If you don't think this is good news, then you may be a bit of a "control freak." Do you really want responsibility for the fulfillment of the kingdom of God? Hello! Not in our job description. We are, at best, seed scatterers. God gives the growth, just as God sends the rain and the sun that makes all growth possible. The Automatic Seed is a humble and, I think, comforting, reminder of our place in the divine and cosmic scheme of things.

The Parable of the Fig Tree:
From the Fig Tree Learn the Parable.

The New Testament has a number of fig trees, some more important than others, and almost all of them have something to do with judgment. Chapter four will focus on parables of judgment, so why talk about fig trees now? Because here, and in the parable of the Wheat and Weeds to follow, the judgment follows the growth, or the lack thereof, before the cutting down and harvesting.

Mark 13:28–31 begins with a peculiar turn of phrase, missed in the NRSV: "From the fig tree learn the parable" is a literal rendering of the phrase. But how is a fig tree a parable? The context is important, as always, and Mark 13 is quite a context. Jesus has been telling his disciples about terrifying events to come, which we have taken to calling the "end times," although that contemporary expression doesn't appear in Scripture. Instead, Jesus builds on the traditions of the prophets, especially Daniel, Isaiah, and Zechariah, to describe events that at first sound a lot like the disaster of war ("nation will rise against nation" [Mark 13:8]), but finally take on a more cosmic coloring ("the sun will be darkened and the moon will not give its light" [Mark 13:24]). The disciples want to know, and we do too, when these things will happen, and while we might wish Jesus said, "March 23, 2009," or something as specific, instead he offers the more cryptic reply:

> "From the fig tree learn its lesson: as soon as its branch becomes tender and puts forth its leaves, you know that summer is near. So also, when you see these things taking place, you know that he is near, at the very gates. Truly I tell you, this generation will not pass away until all these things have taken place. Heaven and earth will pass away, but my words will not pass away." (Mark 13:28–31)

That is certainly clear, isn't it? As surely as a blossoming tree heralds the arrival of summer, the events Jesus describes in Mark 13 herald the coming of the Son of Man. Could it be that simple? I think so, except for two problems. The first is that I am not always sure which biblical fig tree Jesus meant when he said, "From the fig tree learn the parable." The second is that he elsewhere chides the disciples and readers for not being able to rightly apply our reading of Mother Nature to the matters of the Kingdom. First, let's look at the second problem.

In another passage filled with ominous language we now interpret to be about the "end times," Luke includes words of Jesus about the crowd's inability to discern the signs of the times.

> "He also said to the crowds, 'When you see a cloud rising in the west, you immediately say, "It is going to rain"; and so it happens. And when you see the south wind blowing, you say, "There will be scorching heat"; and it happens. You hypocrites! You know how to interpret the appearance of earth and sky, but why do you not know how to interpret the present time?'" (Luke 12:54–56)

If in Luke 12, the ability to interpret the weather is contrasted with the inability to discern the coming of the Kingdom, why is the fig tree in Luke 21:29–30 ("Look at the fig tree . . . as soon as they sprout leaves you can see for yourselves and know that summer is already near") any different? Perhaps because the fig tree is a more significant biblical metaphor, a sign of fruitfulness from the Garden of Eden (those weren't "apple leaves" Adam and Eve used to cover up with) to the Promised Land (Deut 8:8) and beyond. As we will see in chapter four, Jesus uses a cursed fig tree as a symbol of the fate of the Temple in Jerusalem, and in the story now before us, the unfruitful fig tree becomes a symbol of judgment delayed. In chapter six, we will reflect further on how the parables may help us be present and aware of the signs and symbols all around us, but now we have a fig tree to figure out:

> Then he told this parable: "A man had a fig tree planted in his vineyard; and he came looking for fruit on it and found none. So he said to the gardener, 'See here! For three years I have come looking for fruit on this fig tree, and still I find none. Cut it down! Why should it be wasting the soil?' He replied, 'Sir, let it alone for one more year, until I dig around it and put manure on it. If it bears fruit next year, well and good; but if not, you can cut it down.'" (Luke 13:6–9)

If your thumb is as brown as mine, you join me in sympathizing with the fellow in this story. How long must you wait until you get to enjoy the fruit of your labor? It takes a while for the tree to mature to point of yielding edible fruit, and the Torah requires a waiting period until one is permitted to eat up (Lev 19:23). But we assume that this time has passed and the planter now wants to be the eater. Disgusted, he orders the tree to be chopped down, which is sometimes viewed as a spiteful overreaction that deprives the vineyard of the shade the tree provides and prevents the anchoring of the grapevines—the main reason one planted fig trees in vineyards in the first place. Whatever the case, the cooler-headed servant suggests giving the tree another year, with some first-century Miracle-Gro tossed on for good measure. And the owner says. . . . We don't know what the owner says. Jesus never tells us. What do you think happened, and why do you think Jesus told the story? Botanically the argument that more time and added soil nutrients would transform the tree is probably incorrect, and Luke places the story after a rather stinging piece about judgment. The expectation based on biology and context is that the owner would say, "Just do what you are told and chop the thing down." But did he, and why did Jesus leave this decision up to the reader? That is one of the wonderful things about the parables, which Dodd captured in his phrase about "teasing the mind into thought." Just as we do not know what the older brother does at the end of the Prodigal Son, we are allowed, in fact invited, to decide how the parable of the Fig Tree ends. Which makes it difficult to know how to "learn its lesson," but who said this was going to be easy?

Torah is the Hebrew word for law, and is used as shorthand for the "Five Books of Moses"—Genesis through Deuteronomy.

Why did Jesus leave this decision up to the reader?

The Parable of the Wheat and the Tares: The War of the Weeds.

He put before them another parable: "The kingdom of heaven may be compared to someone who sowed good seed in his field; but while everybody was asleep, an enemy came and sowed weeds among the wheat, and then went away. So when the plants came up and bore grain, then the weeds appeared as well. And the slaves of the householder came and said to him, 'Master, did you not sow good seed in your field?

Where, then, did these weeds come from?' He answered, 'An enemy has done this.' The slaves said to him, 'Then do you want us to go and gather them?' But he replied, 'No; for in gathering the weeds you would uproot the wheat along with them. Let both of them grow together until the harvest; and at harvest time I will tell the reapers, Collect the weeds first and bind them in bundles to be burned, but gather the wheat into my barn.'" (Matthew 13:24–30)

If you drive down a suburban side street on a summer day you can spot it—the yard all the neighbors hate. Lush, green, without a weed or brown spot, looking for all the world as if Scott's just filmed a Turf-builder commercial. If you live next door and don't have the time or money to invest in a sprinkler system and monthly Chemlawn visits (and you are not too sure all those chemicals are such a good idea for the ecosystem anyway), you might fantasize about sowing some dandelions and crab grass in the middle of the night, imagining the look on your neighbor's face when his picture-perfect yard sprouts weeds.

Frankly that is the only way I can make sense of Jesus' parable of the Wheat and the Weeds. What kind of "enemy" would do what Jesus described? This is a question that pushes us to the edge of Dodd's "drawn from nature or common life," for it is hard to imagine an enemy pulling what seems more like a prank than an act of war. Not that the action would be without consequence, making extra work for laborers and, if some of the weeds are mistakenly harvested with the wheat, ruining future loaves. But the consequences are not of the life-and-death variety usually associated with the actions of an enemy.

This parable, like the story of the Sower we will consider next, comes with an interpretation, in this case Matt 13:36–43, and like the interpretation of the Sower we will ignore it. We are studying the stories of Jesus, not the interpretations of the stories, even when they're included in Scripture.[7] And, as with the Sower, there is a division of opinion about whether we are dealing with a parable or an allegory, a difference in structure discussed in the next section. I am convinced that while the action pushes our definition of parable to the breaking point, the structure is that of a parable, not an allegory, because there's a central comparison rather than a series of comparisons.

What is the central comparison? That in a way yet to be discerned, the kingdom of heaven is like what a farmer does when finding that the field is a mix of wheat and weeds. How it got that way is not important, so effort spent identifying the enemy is not well spent. The comparison revolves around what the owner decides. When the slaves see that weeds, which agronomists tell us look enough like the wheat to cause problems for the untrained observer, have sprouted alongside the wheat, they are ready to take action. If they were day laborers, you would think they might just be looking for work, for without work there would be no pay, and without pay no dinner that evening. But this would not be the motivation of the slaves, who surely had more than enough work to do, so what exactly was at stake? Just look at the field, for heaven's sake! Everybody knows weeds grow faster, and in the story to follow a similar weed (but two different terms in Greek) will "choke" the sprouting grain. So the decision before the owner of the field was not as simple as it might seem. There were risks involved in waiting, but the owner decided that the risk in weeding was greater, so he waited. And then an interesting detail. The owner says to the slaves, "in gathering the weeds you would uproot the wheat along with them" and so it is best to wait until the harvest, "and at harvest time I will tell the reapers, Collect the weeds first" (Matt 13:29–30). Did you catch it? Not "*you* would uproot the wheat so at the harvest I will tell *you* to gather the weeds first," but "I will tell the *reapers*," who are new to the story. The ones worrying about the weeds will play no role in the harvest. It is also worth noting that the weeds are not simply discarded, but bundled to be used for fuel. The last time I checked, the goal of growing grain is to make bread, and for that you need heat as much as wheat. In an interesting way, then, both weeds and wheat are important.

> What was at stake? Just look at the field, for heaven's sake! Everybody knows weeds grow faster, and in the story to follow a similar weed will "choke" the sprouting grain.

What has any of this have to do with the kingdom of heaven? Any number of things, from patience until the harvest to a distinction between weeders and reapers and the attitude of slaves and owners. Heaven, it seems, can wait. We cannot. We worry about how the field looks or believe that weeds will overwhelm the wheat every time—so for goodness sake somebody do something! But there is nothing *you* can do, no matter where you place yourself in the parable—slaves, owner, even the enemy—nobody does anything until the harvest, and then the ones who act—the reapers—are new to the scene.

You do not need an advanced degree to figure out who the reapers might be. You say "harvest" and I'll say "judgment" every time—the reapers, grim and otherwise, are angels of one sort or another in any end-times scenario I am aware of. What matters most is that who-ever or whatever the reapers are, and whatever it is that they do, it is not something that we ourselves are to do, however much we might like to grab a can of weed killer and have at it.

I think this is wonderfully good news. As much as I might at times like to be the one who separates the weeds and wheat, the sheep and goats, the righteous and the sinner, it is not in my job description. Nor is it in yours or anyone else's who thinks it is. Or did you sup-pose Jesus did not mean it when he said, "Judge not"? (Matt 7:1; Paul and James say the same thing: Rom 2:1, 14:4, and Jas 4:11). This does not mean that we make no distinctions between faithful and sinful behavior, stop teaching our children right from wrong, or close down the Church because it makes no difference whether we serve God or not. It means that the eternal difference it makes is not our decision, and we can stop acting as if it does.

The Story of the Sower: Good Soil Is Hard to Find

"Listen! A sower went out to sow. And as he sowed, some seed fell on the path, and the birds came and ate it up. Other seed fell on rocky ground, where it did not have much soil, and it sprang up quickly, since it had no depth of soil. And when the sun rose, it was scorched; and since it had no root, it withered away. Other seed fell among thorns, and the thorns grew up and choked it, and it yielded no grain. Other seed fell into good soil and brought forth grain, growing up and increasing and yielding thirty and sixty and a hundredfold." And he said, "Let anyone with ears to hear listen!" (Mark 4:3–9).

You go on a picnic in the country one day and find a nice shady spot between a field and a stream. While you are enjoying your lunch and doing a little fishing, someone comes out with a huge bag of seed. At least that's what it looks like, but you can't really be sure and you are not paying that much attention until suddenly the sky is raining seed, all over you and your picnic. "Hey! What do you think you're doing!" you shout, but the sower keeps on sowing. Looking more closely, you notice there is seed everywhere—along the fence-line, down the path toward the stream, in a pile of rocks, among a patch of thistles and a stand of cattails.

More or less that is the scene Jesus describes. Understanding what it means is apparently very important, for when the disciples ask for an explanation Jesus says, "Do you not understand this parable? Then how will you understand all the parables?" (Mark 4:13). At some level the story of the Sower is the interpretive "key" to at least the stories in Mark 4, if not all the stories of Jesus in the Gospel of Mark. Our goal is to find out what that "key" might be.

Readers have wrestled long and hard over the challenges offered by this story, its interpretation found in Mark 4:14–20, and the odd words in Mark 4:9–13 which, as discussed in chapter one, suggest that Jesus spoke in parables so that no one would understand him. While the points of emphasis have differed, we can organize the difficulties in categories familiar from high school English class—structure, character, plot, and meaning.

The structure of the story is a point of contention interesting only to someone who wrote his doctoral dissertation on the topic: me![8] At issue is whether Mark 4:3–9 is a parable or an allegory. The distinction is not great, because both forms use metaphor as the way to make meaning, but over the centuries the complementary relationship of parable and allegory has been lost, and our understanding of the historical Jesus has suffered as a result. The argument goes like this (those who do not want to suffer through a brief encapsulation of my dissertation are invited to skip the five points and paragraph to follow):

- Generations of interpreters insisted that one who spoke in parables would not speak in allegory (Jülicher), so Jesus could not have used allegory in his proclamation.
- If we find something allegorical in the gospels, it was either not spoken by Jesus, or was radically reshaped into its present form by the early church or the Evangelist (Jeremias).
- Mark 4:3–9 must therefore by interpreted as either a parable of Jesus (Crossan and many others), or as an allegory of the early church (Mark 4:14–20; Tolbert[9] and others).
- However, despite the best efforts of many scholars, it is impossible to view the story as a parable, with a central comparison,

when it obviously makes a series of comparisons (the different kinds of soil) and is therefore an allegory.

■ Moreover, the rhetorical distinction between parable and allegory has long been overstated (Aristotle said it was *mikron*), and based on the evidence of the gospels, there is no *rhetorical* basis for denying the form of allegory to the historical Jesus.

Why make such a big deal about whether the story is a parable or an allegory? Primarily because of the impact that decision has on the way we interpret the story. Those who argue that the story is a parable maintain that despite the emphasis in the story on the four different kinds of soil—path, rocks, thorns, and fertile—there is really only a single contrast, between fruitful and unfruitful. A variety of arguments, including the ever-popular search for the "original" story of Jesus "underneath" the gospel text, are marshaled, all foundering on the simple fact that the story distinguishes in vivid detail three different kinds of unfruitful soil. While some go so far as to suggest a radically reworked text to support their views, in recent years the tide has turned both in favor of the text as we have it in Mark, and in support of reading that text as an allegory. New Testament scholar Mary Ann Tolbert offered a compelling reading of the story as allegory, a reading I fault only for being limited to the world of the gospel, seeing Mark 4:3–9 and later Mark 12:1–10 as allegories outlining the gospel story to be told in the chapters that follow. On one level she is correct, but as we will see shortly the Allegory of the Seed and Soil is not just about the reception of Jesus' message in the Gospel of Mark, it is a question of character.

The question of character in the story is complicated by the fact that there are really not any. The sower disappears so quickly that his or her character must not be of central importance, despite years of reading the story as if somewhere, either in the story itself or the interpretation a few verses later, we are told, "the sower is Jesus." In Mark 4:3–9 it is as if the seed sows itself, just as the seeds grow automatically in Mark 4:26–29. The search for characters to talk about has led many to personify the soils, with Tolbert going so far as to name them—the rocky soil is Peter (*petros*) and the thorny soil the rich young man in chapter 10:17–22. This is succes-

> The question of character in the story is complicated by the fact that there are really not any.

ful so long as one stays only within the world of the gospel, but captures neither what the allegory would have meant to Jesus' hearers nor what it might mean to those who read it today. In a way, the central question of character remains the question of the identity of the sower, whose role is too limited to represent Jesus but must surely represent someone.

> **Personification** is the literary device of treating an inanimate object, such as soil, weeds, and so on, as if they were people—believers or scoffers perhaps.

The plot of the allegory is one of its most intriguing elements. On the surface the plot is simple: a sower scatters seed, most of it fails to produce any fruit, but the seed that lands in fertile ground produces abundantly. Yet as the text reports, and as slightly reworked in the version with which this section began, it seems to me we have here either the story of the dumbest farmer in history, or a story about something else besides farming. Why, especially in a world of poverty and scarcity, where presumably every seed was precious, would a sower cast seed in places where it had no chance to grow? Interpreters including Jeremias and Bailey have referred to a practice of plowing after sowing, an interesting if largely undocumented claim that stumbles on one slight problem: the story does not mention plowing. The only conclusion seems to be that the sower knowingly casts seed in places where it is not likely to grow, and where, if it does grow, finally does not produce fruit. What is that about?

Which brings us to meaning. To recall what we've said before, the story is structured as an allegory, making a series of comparisons, or metaphors, to generate its meaning. The identity of the sower remains in question, as does the reason for the action of sowing seed where it is not likely to sprout, grow, or produce fruit. Our answer to these questions is important; the text, after all, suggests that if we cannot understand this story we likely cannot understand the rest.[10]

My reading focuses on the sower, particularly the significance of the sower's anonymity. This anonymity suggests the sower could be just about anyone. Exactly. The interpretation of the allegory found in Mark 4:14–20 begins, "The sower sows the word," and "word" is as loaded a term in Mark as it is in the Gospel of John and elsewhere in the early Christian tradition (Mark 2:2; 1 Thess 1:6; Jas 1:22; Heb 4:12, to give four examples from around the tradition). Just as in the interpretation, the focus in the allegory moves immediately from the sower to the seed in the various soils, the seed/word taking on more importance than the sower. That could not be true if the sower is Jesus. But it could be true if sower is you, or me.

The allegory of the sower is not an encouragement to be fertile soil, but to be sowers of the word, in particular to be sowers of the word without regard to the potential fruitfulness of the soil in which the seed/word is cast. In vivid detail the story describes the fate of three groups of seed and soil, each description "drawn from nature or the common life," in this instance not that the listeners saw someone sowing in the rocks, thorns, and path, but that they could easily imagine what would happen to seed sown in such unpromising places. The strangeness is the impossibility of imagining a sower who would intentionally waste the seed. "And so teasing the mind into active thought," we come to the conclusion that the story is not about farming, it is about evangelism.[11]

How much one emphasizes the series of unsuccessfully sown seed, and the significance of the soil into which the seed is sown, will vary from time to time and place to place. Certainly the church in the first century of its existence on to the present has been right to see the experience of failed evangelism in the path, rocks, and thorns. Tolbert was also right to recognize that Mark used the allegory as a "story within the story" to prepare the reader for what was to come. But we are just as correct to see the allegory working more generally, and by describing more widely the experience of evangelism also encouraging the hearer/reader to be a sower. The allegory is polyvalent—it has multiple meanings.

What should the reader do with the multiple meanings in the allegory? Put it to work. First, by recognizing that Jesus is inviting us to think of ourselves not as soil, but as sowers—as evangelists, as sharers of the good news of God's love for the world in Jesus Christ, we sow the word, and the word we sow is more important than we are ourselves. Second, while recognizing that not every sowing will be productive also realizing that is not our concern, nor should it keep us from casting the seed every which way. Admittedly our own "nature or common life" might not best be pictured as path, rocks, and thorns, but we have our own analogs, and our own temptation to hold onto our

> Jesus is inviting us to think of ourselves not as soil, but as sowers—as evangelists, as sharers of the good news of God's love for the world.

seed (the word) until we find the occasion that seems to hold the greatest promise of a fruitful response.

We could imagine a college dorm, a prison chapel, an impoverished neighborhood, and a church retreat center. Likely the best spot to gain a good hearing for the gospel would be the retreat center, because that is what people there expect to hear. But do we really want to limit our sharing of the gospel to the retreat center? Might not the dorm or the prison or the neighborhood turn out to have ears ready to hear? And even if they do not, should we then not try?

Okay, you are thinking, that makes some sense. The sower is not Jesus, the soils are places or opportunities to share the word about Jesus, some that seem promising and some that do not, and my responsibility is not to worry so much about which occasion seems the best but to share the good news all over the place. But what about the multiple yields? Is "one hudred-fold" a lot? And how does any of this provide a key to understanding other parables and allegories of Jesus?

Good questions, so I hope you like the answers. The increasing yields do, on one level, correspond to the three failed soils, the thirty, sixty, hundred matching the path, rocks, and thorns. Allegory likes parallelism as much as parable. Is one hundred-fold a lot? In our day, with hybrid seed, fertilizer, irrigation, and mechanized reaping, probably not. In Jesus' day it probably was. But was it a miraculous yield? What little evidence we have suggests that it was not, so the yield is best viewed as abundant but not spectacular.

So where's the key? You are. If this reading is persuasive (as opposed to "right," a category that presumes there is only one way to read the story, the opposite of the polyvalent approach I advocate), it suggests that the reader finds an unlikely place for him or herself, as an actor, not as one acted upon. We are not soil, called to be fertile, we are sowers, called to sow with abandon. When applying this "key" to the mustard seed and the seed growing automatically, we imagine ourselves having the expansive potential of the mustard grain, and often growing in spite of ourselves. To apply this key to a popular parable chapter, Luke 15, to be considered in chapter three, think of the story of the Lost Sheep (vv. 4–6). We have an almost instinctive interpretation—that's me! I'm the lost sheep! Jesus, good shepherd that you are, come and find me! We carry this with us to our reading of the story of the

Prodigal, which soon follows, remembering our every sin and fault and seeing ourselves in the younger son. The problem is that between the Lost Sheep and the Lost Son is the story of the Lost Coin. Materialistic as our culture is, few of us imagine ourselves as a coin lost under the bed, praying to be swept into view by the divine domestic. But if we are not the lost coin, perhaps we are neither lost sheep nor lost son. Could these familiar stories, when we look where the action is, result in different interpretations? I think they do, and I think the "key" taken from the Allegory of the Seed and Soil will help us discover those interpretations. We will try it out in the chapters to follow.

The Kingdom of God Is Like . . .

Which brings us to our first opportunity to ponder how we should understand the "kingdom of God" that is the topic of so many of the parables. Obviously it is not a spatial location, although the word forces us to think of it as a place of some sort or another. Most recent interpreters have moved away from the patriarchal and hierarchical imagery of KINGdom to instead speak of "reign" or "rule" of God, and that is certainly a step in the right direction. What we have seen in the stories encountered in this chapter is that the "kingdom" is first of all a place of activity, kingdom is in some way a verb, so "reign" works very well. But the "reigning" is not limited to God, not if we are to be sowers. Nor, as important as the action is, do we do everything in this kingdom—we are not, for an important example, the reapers. The kingdom of God therefore is a dynamic in which we share a way of living. We will come back to this.

Continuing the Conversation . . .

As noted Brandon Scott makes regular and significant use of the *Gospel of Thomas* in his interpretation of the parables (*Hear Then the Parable* (Minneapolis: Fortress Press, 1989). For a copy of the *Gospel of Thomas* the most ready reference is *The Nag Hamadi Library in English*, edited by James M. Robinson (San Francisco: Harper SanFrancisco, 1990), which includes a host of early Christian and gnostic noncanonical writings originally in Coptic.

Those interested in the many agricultural parables of Jesus, and in what they may say about "everyday life in Bible times" will particularly enjoy the interpretations of Kenneth Bailey in *Poet and Peasant* and *Through Peasant Eyes*, two volumes now available as one (Grand Rapids: Eerdmans, 1983).

CHAPTER THREE

Seek Ye First: Parables of Seeking

"Finding is the first act," begins the poem,[1] though in fact, seeking is the first act. After chiding for worrying about the wrong things, Jesus said, "Seek first the kingdom" (Matt 6:33—I have no idea why the NRSV chose to translate the Greek word as "strive"), and common sense tells us that you have to look before you can find. So seeking is the first act, and seeking is the focus of many of our favorite parables. There is always an exception that proves the rule—in this case, a parable that begins with finding.

The Treasure and the Pearl: Finders Keepers

"The kingdom of heaven is like treasure hidden in a field, which someone found and hid; then in his joy he goes and sells all that he has and buys that field." (Matthew 13:44)

- The kingdom is like a treasure. (That's easy enough.)
- The kingdom is like treasure hidden in a field. (Buried treasure, that sounds like fun.)
- The kingdom is like buried treasure which someone finds. (Okay, that still makes sense.)
- The kingdom of heaven is like buried treasure that someone finds and hides. (That's a little weird, but I am still with you.)

- The kingdom is like buried treasure that someone finds, hides, and happily goes and sells everything she has. (That is more than a little weird; that is downright strange.)
- The kingdom is like buried treasure that someone finds, hides, joyfully sells everything and buys the field in which the treasure is buried. (You lost me.)

The Greek text of this parable is only thirty-one words long, but a lot happens. Why it happens, how it happens, and whether or not it should happen is what we need to consider.

Our definition of parable says that it should be "drawn from nature or common life," and we have already seen that this means the common life of 2,000 years ago, with which we must familiarize ourselves to make the best sense of the story. So how common was buried treasure in ancient Palestine? More common than you would think.

Let's say you inherited a tidy sum back in the first century of our era. Where would you put it? In an agrarian society of clans and villages where everybody knew everybody else's business, everyone knows that you are wealthier than you were yesterday, and not everybody would necessarily be happy about it. There is not a bank to go to unless you happened to live in a major city, no mattress to stuff (and those coins would be lumpy anyway), and no place to hide it in your simple one- or two-room house. You could dig up a spot on your dirt floor and hide it there, but how hard would that be for someone else to find while you are out working in the field? So you hide it in your field one day when folks think you are roughing up the ground before the spring planting. Before too long the plants in the field have blossomed and your carefully chosen spot looks to all the world like every other spot in the field.

Of course it may also look like every other spot in the field to you too, which is one explanation for how someone might have left a treasure behind in the first place. Or it could have been that the Romans swept through one day and you had to flee before having time to retrieve your treasure. Maybe you saved it for a rainy day that never came, maybe you got mad at your kids and decided not to tell them where it was hidden, knowing that if they would just get off their lazy behinds and get to work it would be their plow that bumped into the box of silver one day.

In any case, we have buried treasure that someone finds, apparently by accident because the story does not say that the kingdom was like someone *looking* for treasure in a field. Who would that be? Not those lazy kids, that's for sure, because they would not need to buy the field—they already owned it. Someone else, perhaps a day laborer, or an overseer or steward, or someone enjoying a moment of incredible luck digging for worms to fish with. We know only one thing for sure about who it was: someone who did not have legal right to what had been found. Finders may be keepers and possesion nine-tenths of the law, but legally, then as now, what was found was the property of the owner of the field, not the finder.

Finders may be keepers and possesion nine-tenths of the law, but legally, then as now, what was found was the property of the owner of the field, not the finder.

Which explains why the finder reburied the treasure, sold his or her own property and possessions, and bought the field. By most accounts this made the finder the keeper, legally, but what about morally? If the kingdom of heaven is like finding, reburying, selling, and buying, is the kingdom of heaven, at best, a little sneaky, and at worse, duplicitous?

The answer turns on whether the reader feels the finder had responsibility to inform the owner of the field what had been discovered. It is obvious that the owners did not know about the treasure, otherwise they would have either refused the sale or reclaimed the treasure before the property changed hands. Can you steal something from someone when they do not know they own it?

This reading has been faulted for being overly fussy, focusing on legal and moral niceties and missing the central dynamic of the joy at discovering treasure. Perhaps. But Jesus did not tell a simple story—just a short, complicated one. Had "joy in the finding" been the only dynamic Jesus intended, then the finder would have discovered the treaure in property he or she already owned. In a story crafted as carefully as this one, a detail like the finder not owning the field was hardly an oversight. It adds an element of moral ambiguity that must be addressed, which we will do after looking at the second short parable of finding with which the treasure in the field is paired, The Pearl:

> "Again, the kingdom of heaven is like a merchant in search of fine pearls; on finding one pearl of great value, he went and sold all that he had and bought it." (Matt 13:45–46)

Only twenty-five words in Greek, The Pearl is nevertheless a full and rich parable, similar to The Treasure but different in interesting and important ways. The protagonist is called a merchant. While merchants made only rare (and almost never positive) appearances in the New Testament (cf. Rev 18), they're mentioned often enough (e.g. Jas 4) to be familiar characters to Jesus' hearers and Matthew's readers. The kingdom is being compared to a pearl trader, who makes a living by selling pearls for more than he paid for them. Is this exploitation of those who dive for pearls? Perhaps, but we had plenty of moral ambiguity in the previous story, too.

How far and wide the merchant traveled is not known, for pearls were to be found in the Red Sea and Persian Gulf, and more famously in the Indian Ocean. The ancient historian Pliny describes pearls as the most precious of all objects,[2] while Job describes wisdom as so valuable as to be above the price of pearls (Job 28:18).[3] A pearl trader would have sounded exciting, but not entirely foreign. Those are "pearly" gates in heaven, after all (Rev 21:21). The dynamic of the story is straightforward. A merchant finds a special pearl in the course of his trading, and, like the one who found the treasure in the field, sells all that he has in order to acquire it. No mention of joy is made in this story, perhaps because the transaction was just a matter of business.

Here is the main question: What did the merchant do with the pearl once it had been acquired at the cost of everything he owned? Put it on the mantel? Apparently not, because the mantel would have been sold along with everything else. The merchant could not eat the pearl, and he could not sleep underneath it. Unless he charged admission to come and look at the beautiful pearl, he would have soon starved and died, just as the finder of the treasure in the field would have done without having sold it. Clearly, then, the merchant sold the pearl. That's right—the merchant sold the beautiful pearl for which she/he had sold everything. It's what merchants do. And likely made a fortune in the process.

You may have noticed that I am reading way beyond the narratives themselves, not something I encourage, but at times it's necessary in order not to miss the dynamic of the story. Jesus did not say the kingdom of heaven was a treasure or a pearl, he said the kingdom was like finding and buying the field and the pearl. The treasure and the pearl had to have been quickly liquidated at great profit, or our two finders would have been goners. It is the process of finding, not the objects found, that is key. Those who say that these two parables teach us to make any sacrifice, give up whatever is asked, so that we may enter the kingdom of heaven, misunderstand the stories. In them, there is no sacrifice, and no possession—just an arguably shady transaction (buying the field) and a sound business move (acquiring the pearl). What do these actions have to do with the kingdom of heaven?

That we are talking about actions, not objects, is very important. The kingdom is not something we possess, like a treasure or pearl, however valuable those may be. As we saw at the end of chapter two, the kingdom in these stories seems to be better understood as something we do, or a way that we live. Both finders take decisive action, one with joy and the somewhat questionable course of reburying the treasure and buying the field without disclosing the presence of the treasure, the other with a sure business sense, perhaps buying the pearl with a collector in mind to whom he would soon sell it. The stories serve to illustrate what Jesus meant when he elsewhere says, "Be wise as serpents and innocent as doves" (Matt 10:16). That our models might be described as a lucky rogue and a shrewd business person is not insignificant either. These are not often the types lifted up in sermon and speech to inspire the faithful, but Jesus populated his stories, and his supper table, with just such folk. It is time to meet a few more.

That we are talking about actions, not objects, is very important. The kingdom is not something we possess, like a treasure or pearl, it seems to be more about something we do, a way that we live.

The Lost Sheep: Leave Them Alone and They Don't Always Come Home

It is hard to pick a subject that seems more drawn from nature and common life than sheep. Psalm 23 tells us the Lord is our shepherd; in John 10 Jesus says that he is the good shepherd; in Matt 9:36 Jesus has compassion for the crowd because they seem "like sheep without a shepherd." The sheep is an important metaphor in the tradition, but one that does not stand up well to overly exacting analysis. Sheep, after all, are generally described as stupid and smelly, and as the old joke goes, a pastor shepherds the sheep for one of two reasons: to fleece them or eat them.

The parable of the Lost Sheep is known to us in two slightly different versions in Scripture, Matt 18:12–14 and Luke 15:4–7 (there is also a version in the *Gospel of Thomas*, an important witness to the Jesus tradition written, I think, after the gospels and not included in our canon, or this book). We will look at Luke's account, because it is the first of three parables of seeking in Luke 15—lost sheep, lost coin, lost son. The story, removed from its setting (a dispute with scribes and Pharisees) and summary application telling the reader what it means (a kind of "nah, nah, nah, nah, nah/angels like sinners better than they like you guys"), is typically short and sweet.

> Which one of you, having a hundred sheep and losing one of them, does not leave the ninety-nine in the wilderness and go after the one that is lost until he finds it? When he has found it, he lays it on his shoulders and rejoices. And when he comes home, he calls together his friends and neighbors, saying to them, "Rejoice with me, for I have found my sheep that was lost." (Luke 15:4–6)

Every church more than thirty years old has the picture somewhere in or near the nursery: Jesus carrying a lamb on his shoulder, and that picture has probably done more to influence our interpretation of the parable than all the books and sermons ever written. (A Google search turned up 1,260 versions of the image on the Internet.) The context in Luke, an argument over who Jesus hangs out with, and by extension, who is welcome in the kingdom, is important but not for this conversation, which is more interested in the meaning of the parable than in its meaning in Luke's gospel. And on the basis of the story alone we have a problem, because the answer to the question with which the story begins, "Which of you . . . does not leave the ninety-nine?" is, "None of us!"

Our shepherd and sheep are in the wilderness, or desert. This is not only an inhospitable environment, it is a biblically scary spot, where Jesus is tempted (Mark 1:12) and John the Baptist rants (Mark 1:4), and to which scapegoats are dispatched (Lev 16:10). We should assume there are predators, thieves, ghosts, and goblins in abundance. If we include ourselves in the "Which of you?" then we must imagine ourselves out in the wilderness with our one hundred sheep, not a flock of Jacobean proportions but not bad. One of the flock slips away, which can only mean that it's gone further into the desert, for had it stumbled back toward the village it would not be described as lost. Here is our choice—do we leave ninety-nine sheep unguarded in the desert and take off after the lost one, or do we accept a one percent loss as an acceptable cost of doing business because the desert is no place to leave ninety-nine percent of our livelihood to fend for itself?

That is an easy choice, so when the shepherd takes off after the stray, we have strayed into Dodd's "arrests the hearer by its vividness or strangeness," and we begin to think this shepherd must be related to the sower who tosses seed onto rocks and into the weeds. Still, let's not be too harsh, because as luck would have it, the shepherd finds the stray. Hooray! Now he can hurry back to the ninety-nine, give the lost sheep a good talking to on the way, and all's well that ends well. Except our shepherd doesn't go back to the others, he goes home and apparently throws a party. "Rejoice with me, for I have found my sheep that was lost." The way this story is going, the shepherd probably roasted the lost/found sheep and served it to his neighbors during the celebration.

I mentioned the sower for a reason, to recall the interpretive key found in reading the Allegory of the Seed and Soil (Mark 4:3–9): look for the action. Most traditional readings of the Lost Sheep assume that it offers an illustration of Psalm 23, with Jesus as shepherd and the readers as sheep. This allows us to acknowledge our waywardness and need for a shepherd and guide. It also lets us off the hook and misses the focus of the story. Jesus did not say, "Which of you, having wandered away from the flock in the wilderness, hopes that the shepherd will come and find you?" But that is the traditional way of reading the parable, our nursery room picture front and center. Using the key found in Mark 4, and attending to the story Jesus told, we have no choice but to take our responsibility as shepherds, and we must decide whether we will look for the lost sheep or play it safe, and smart, and protect the ninety-nine.

If we are honest, we admit our intention to cut our losses, call Lassie, and bring the ninety-nine back to town. It is tempting (having mentioned the possibility of a sheep dog) to suggest that when the shepherd looks for the lost sheep there are other shepherds, dogs, or at least a young boy herder or two to watch the ninety-nine. But these are no more in the story than Lassie. And we cannot ignore the fact that the way Jesus tells the story it is obvious he thinks we are supposed to do what we do not want to do—look for the lost one and, for some reason yet to be determined, when we find the lost sheep, continue to ignore the rest of the flock and have a party to celebrate finding the one.

Luke makes it almost impossible to read the parable of the Lost Sheep without having the two stories that follow, the Lost Coin and Lost Son, in mind. Later in the gospel Jesus will say, "The Son of Man came to seek out and to save the lost" (19:10), tempting us back into the role of lost sheep. But not in Luke 15. Here, like it or not, we are the seekers, and while it is not the most obvious rhetorical strategy, in Luke 15 we are challenged to begin our seeking in the wilderness, and to do it at great risk to ourselves and our security. In an important way, the shepherd is indeed as crazy as the sower, and the action reckless, even foolish. Is Jesus saying that sometimes we must take risks, go to places we would rather not go, do and say things well outside our comfort zone? Yes, and he's also saying that this will be the source of considerable joy, for ourselves and for others.

The Lost Coin: A Penny Saved

One of the important things about Luke's positioning of the story of the Lost Coin is that it corrects our tendency to see ourselves as the lost, rather than as the seeker, before we get to the most famous parable of all, the Prodigal. While we may think of ourselves as many things, we do not imagine ourselves a coin.

> Or what woman having ten silver coins, if she loses one of them, does not light a lamp, sweep the house, and search carefully until she finds it? When she has found it, she calls together her friends and neighbors, saying, "Rejoice with me, for I have found the coin that I had lost." (Luke 15:8–9)

Here we have something embarrassingly unusual, a woman as protagonist in a parable. Women are rarely present as characters in Jesus' stories, but when they are, such as here and in the parable of the Persistent Widow (Luke 18:1–8), we have much to learn. The dynamic is enough like that of the Lost Sheep to form a pattern that will also be followed in the story of the Prodigal. A coin is lost; it represents ten percent of a woman's wealth, which was not much—a drachma, roughly equivalent to a denarius in value, was worth only one day's wage. Ten days' wages is a paycheck, not a fortune, but it was more security than most had then, and for that matter, than most in the world have now. More to the point, the loss of one tenth of even a tiny fortune is still well worth the search. The little details— lighting a lamp, sweeping, and seeking diligently—simply but surely demonstrate the thoroughness of the search. More interesting is the phrase "until she finds it." It was never a matter of if, but when. And then, like the shepherd, she throws a party. "Rejoice with me!" One wonders if the party cost more than a drachma.

Following our strategy of interpretation, the reader is encouraged to focus on the action of the woman, not in the details but in the larger pattern of seeking, finding, and rejoicing. In an interesting way, which will require more comment in the next section, while the woman was not required to take a risk as great as did the shepherd, more was at stake—ten percent of her wealth, not one percent of her flock. This trend will increase, and it will come to seem that the closer to home we must seek, the more we have to lose. It is also important that while the call in the story of the Lost Coin to be a seeker close to home appears less risky than searching in the wilderness, it requires no less diligence, and evokes the same joyous response. Sometimes we seek in hard-to-reach, potentially dangerous places, and some-times we look around the corner or under the couch, but the joy in the finding is equally sweet.

Something else about the joy is well worth noting: in both stories the joy is shared. The good news of finding is too wonderful to keep to oneself; it must be shared. Truly shared. Not rejoice *for* me, but rejoice *with* me, which suggests an active role for friends and neighbors. We call this community—being together in joy, and also sorrow, seeking, and whatever else life brings. Experiences of community are precious, and are nurtured by sharing joy. The sharing is not always easy, especially when the joy seems to be based on someone else's good fortune. Why should *I* rejoice when something wonderful happens to *you*? It did *me* no good, just you. That attitude may be exactly why experiences of community are so rare. We expect others to

The good news of finding is too wonderful to keep to yourself, it must be shared. Truly shared. Not rejoice for me, but rejoice with me.

rejoice in our good fortune, but have no idea why we should rejoice in theirs.

The joy of community is joy in others, joy in sharing, and joy in living for something other than ourselves. We are not very good at that—our calculators are only useful for measuring the material, while the spiritual, lacking quantification, is dismissed as insignificant, even though life frequently reminds us that we cannot find what we want in ourselves alone, that we need others because we were made for others. Even a misanthrope needs friends.

The linguistic root of the word translated in Luke 15:6 and 9 as "rejoice" is the Greek word *charis*, which when rendered as *chairō* means "rejoice" and as *sunchairō* means "rejoice with." But *charis* itself means "grace," in many respects the most theologically important word in the New Testament. *Charis* is the gracious gift of God that distinguishes joy from happiness, the grace that makes a small coin a subject of eternal significance. The foundation of our joy, and of community, is in the grace of God, a grace that transforms in the giving, not just the receiving.

One drachma is no big deal? You bet it is. Rejoice!

The Lost Son: The Grace of Small Things

Luke 15:11–32 is both the longest and best known of all Jesus' parables, celebrated in art, literature, music, books, and sermons. Lots of sermons. The story is complex and compelling, and depending on the character we focus on, its interpretation can be quite varied. We know from the context that Luke understood the parable to relate in some way to Jesus' practice of open table fellowship ("This fellow welcomes sinners and eats with them" Luke 15:2), and that by his placement of the stories of the Lost Sheep and Lost Coin, Luke has provided a striking setting. Like most preachers, over the years I have come to some very different conclusions about the message of the Prodigal Son, so all we can say about what follows is that as of this writing, it represents my most faithful interpretation of a fascinating story. The parable is too long (the NRSV is 514 words) to reproduce in full, but likely it is familiar enough for a synopsis to suffice.

The younger son of a man with substantial property decides to strike out on his own, and asks for the portion of his family's property to which he will be entitled at his father's death to be given to him. He hits the road apparently wanting to get as far from home as possible, and "squanders his property in dissolute living" (the Greek word, *asōtōs*, suggests reckless and immoral activity). Flat broke in a foreign land, he takes a job that was even lower in pay than in prestige, slopping the hogs, and was so hungry he began to envy the swine their swill. He "came to himself" (15:17) and decided that as long as he didn't have anything to eat he might as well swallow his pride, go home, and ask for a job alongside his father's servants. He practices a speech on the way but never gets a chance to make the whole thing, for when his father sees him, he runs to greet him, kisses him, and orders fresh clothing, sandals, and a ring be brought, and a grand welcome-home party begins. Big brother is finishing his day's work when the reunion occurs, and by the time he gets home, the party is in full swing and he is in high dudgeon, refusing to join the festivities. Dad comes out to ask him in, explaining why he is rejoicing, and reaffirms the elder brother's status. But the story ends with no indication that the brother's mind is changed.

There is much to unpack, and while I am as fond of chronological order as the next person, it may prove best to instead look at the pivotal characters in the order of narrative importance, that is, who gets the most space in the story. So let's look at the brothers first, and then turn our attention to Dad.

I'll start by putting in a good word for the older brother, which, since I am the younger of two siblings, will surprise my sister, Sylvia. We have already mentioned that it is hard to rejoice with others over *their* good fortune. Somehow most of us do not seem to be wired that way when it comes to our neighbors and friends. And when it comes to our sisters and brothers, just remember how the first pair of biblical siblings turned out ("Cain rose up against his brother Abel, and killed him," Genesis 4:8). So before we cast aspersions at the sanctimonious and jealous attitude of the prodigal's brother, let's ask ourselves one thing: What exactly did he do wrong? Work too hard? He claims and his father accepts that he has always done everything asked of him (15:29), so we are really down on the older brother for his attitude, which is probably more than a little hypocritical on *our* part. All the older brother did was refuse to pretend that he was happy about the party now being given for his sibling, and even that unhappiness may have been only for a short while. Okay, there is the matter of his unkind speculation that "this son of yours" (not, significantly, "my brother") had "devoured your property with prostitutes" (15:30), a conclusion only suggested by the word "dissolute" in verse 13, and in any case a bit of information to which he had no access. But beyond the harsh words, I don't think the older brother deserves to be the poster boy for everything pompously pious in Christian tradition. In fact, I find one phrase sadly endearing—"You have never given me even a young goat so that I might celebrate with my friends" (15:29). We will come back to this soon.

The late and beloved baseball relief pitcher Tug McGraw, father of the even more famous country singer, said, when asked after winning the World Series how he would spend his share of bonus, "Ninety percent of it I'll spend on wine, women, and song. The rest I'll probably waste." If only the younger son had held on to ten percent. But he didn't—in fact, he didn't do much of anything right in the entire story. So why are most readers harder on the older than the younger brother? Look at what the younger brother did *and* said. "Dad, I can't wait until you are dead—I want my cut of the inheritance now." Then he took off, without leaving a forwarding address, to a place as far away as he could get. Luke doesn't tell us that he shook the dust off his feet when he left, but you sort of get that feeling.

> "Ninety percent of it I'll spend on wine, women, and song. The rest I'll probably waste."

It's funny how young people, and even young adults, are about money. We try to explain to our teenage daughter that we cannot always afford to do what she wants (her desires often involve overseas travel), and her response is, "I'll help." Given that her major source of income is still the allowance we provide, it is a nice thought but not much more. Until you first try to pay all the bills on what you yourself have earned, you don't understand how expensive it is to be on your own. So it is not hard to imagine that the younger son thought the wad of cash in his pocket would last forever, and while we are not told how long he held out, my guess is weeks rather than months; certainly not years.

At that point, he had worked himself into a very tight corner, for by demanding his share of the family's wealth he had in an odd way disinherited himself. He was not entitled to any more; in fact, he was not entitled to what was given to him until his father died, but that is a topic to consider later. And it appears that he made a bad choice of a "distant country" to settle in, because no sooner had he spent his last drachma than the bottom fell out of the economy and a famine resulted. (As much fun as it would be to join the older brother in speculating on exactly what "dissolute living" consists of, there is not enough textual basis for doing so.)

Even when the younger brother wanted to, he could not find an honest job at decent pay. In desperation he "hired himself out to a citizen of that country" (v. 15), a translation that is probably overly generous. The RSV reads "joined himself," which has the overtones of bonded servitude the Greek verb conveys, and helps make sense of his decision when he "came to himself," an expression itself needing some explanation. This was not a come-to-Jesus moment; this was someone giving himself a dope slap. Put more formally, his hunger and his servitude led to a moment of clarity, and he realized that if he was going to work for chicken feed—or worse, for pig food—he might as well work for his father, whose "hired hands have bread enough and to spare" (v. 17). Enlightened self-interest, not religious conversion, is behind his decision.

On the way home he practices his "I'm sorry" speech. It is filled with bowing and scraping ("I have sinned against heaven and before you"), pathos and groveling ("I am no longer worthy to be called your son"). Legally, he is quite correct. By taking his inheritance before his father's death, he is no longer entitled to the rights of a son, and given his work history, he will be lucky to get any job at all. So there you have it—a young rascal who runs through his inheritance before his father has even died finds that he cannot support himself, and is now crawling back to ask for forgiveness and an entry-level job. And *this* is the brother folks would prefer to be identified with? Not today, and certainly not in Jesus' day. The people listenting to Jesus tell the story would have been hoping the father gives the wayward son just what he had coming. Leviticus 20:9 requires taking the life of one who curses father or mother—one way to see what the younger son did by asking for his inheritance before his father's death. And there's always Deut 27:16, "Cursed be anyone who dishonors father or mother." The younger son certainly did that.

Which brings us to Dad. My great parable teacher, John R. Donahue, S.J., reminded us in class that the story begins "A certain man had two sons" and the Apostles' Creed describes Jesus as God's "only son our Lord," so whoever this story is about, it is not about God. We will come back to that soon. The Dad in our story was a rich man, with land to divide, slaves and hired workers, fatted calves, extra sets of clothes, even a gold ring or two to spare. There are actually lots of rich men in Jesus' parables (Rich Fool in Luke 12, Rich Man and Lazarus and the Dishonest Steward's boss in Luke 16, the Vineyard Owner in Matt 20, to name a few), and income disparities in ancient Palestine were extreme—the rich got richer back then too, so the story of a rich man would have been part of the "common life." Would the people have been jealous? Not as the story unfolded, because the man's money only seemed to create the conditions for his misery.

What was the father like? Lately, he has been taking quite a beating. He's described as the head of a dysfunctional family, playing favorites and creating sibling rivalry between his sons, lacking the decency to tell the older son his brother was home, and failing to invite him to the party before it started. He has even been described as abusive, forcing his older son to work while others celebrate, demanding obedience but failing to reward it with so much as a goat. Whew.

I have been blessed with only one child, but that is more than enough experience to give me a little sympathy for other parents. It is a tough, wonderful, and incredibly important job, the most important and wonderful job God has given me. Two kids, especially boys, would probably kill me. So we need to find somewhere between calling the father "God" and making him into an abusive father. Maybe that is why I like to call him Dad, to see him as a typical parent with love for his children, but also often clueless when it comes to the effect his actions have on his kids, and the reason for their rivalries.

I am not buying the idea that he played favorites. In fact, the narrative describes him, in quite remarkable language, as going out to both sons. "But while he was still far off, his father saw him and was filled with compassion; he ran and put his arms around him and kissed him" (15:20); "His father came out and began to plead with him" (15:28). He has compassion for the younger and beseeches the older—passionate words indeed. This does not mean he didn't treat the younger brother in an extraordinary way: running down the road, publicly displaying affection, and, far from calling down a curse on the boy, restoring him to a place of honor (robe and sandals) and inheritance (ring). He did not do the same thing for the older because those things were already in place. Did he wait too long to go out to the older son? Psychologically, I suppose so, but the narrative required that we have a separate scene. Imagine the story if the father had instead taken his long-lost son out to the fields and called the elder over to greet him, given what we know from the dynamics in the story as we have it: is there any reason to think a more prompt invitation to the party would have made much difference? I for one don't think so. Sibling rivalries don't die that quickly.

Dad makes some noteworthy decisions we should consider further before stepping back and looking at the story as a whole and in the context in which Jesus and Luke placed it. A couple of verses from Hebrew Scripture suggest that the legal norm, if not actual practice, was a considerably different set of responses to the requests of the sons. While there is some evidence that younger sons often set off to seek their fortune elsewhere because the vast majority of the family's wealth goes to the eldest as a way of keeping the patrimony intact, there is no evidence that the father was in any way required to parcel out his property as if he were dead. In retrospect, he probably regretted doing so, but he did not want the young man to go out into the world with nothing. I like to think of it as the ancient equivalent of giving your kids a credit card when they head off to college, saying, "Only use this in an emergency" and discovering when the first bill arrives what a different definition of "emergency" is in effect on campus than at home. The attribution of compassion when he sees his son coming up the road is significant, for compassion is a rare term in the New Testament, used to describe the deepest possible emotion. Luke, for example, also used it to describe the Samaritan's response on seeing the wounded man beside the road (ch. 10) and Jesus' concern for the widow in Nain before he raises her son (ch. 7). Compassion trumps Torah, and rather than being cast off, cursed, or at least chastised, the well-rehearsed "I'm sorry" speech is overwhelmed by embrace. Finally, I again emphasize that the father "went out" to the elder son just as he did to the younger. He didn't send a servant with a demand that his son obediently put in an appearance at the party, but went to him himself and pleaded, reminding the elder son that "all that is mine is yours" (v. 31). What more could he do? In fact, the most amazing thing the father did is nothing at all.

When you bring Dad and his two sons into view at the same time, something that never happens in the parable, what do you have? You have a family: messy, passionate, sometimes self-serving and often held together only by the parents' love (I don't know where Mom is in this story). This is not an ideal family, just a family. Wealthy, but what good did that do? The younger son squandered what he was given and the older resented it as much as he resented that his brother was welcomed back. But this isn't the only time one child ever complained that the parent was not fair, treated the children differently, played favorites, and let the younger one get away with murder. It happened in my family. How about yours?

> When you bring Dad and his two sons into view at the same time, something that never happens in the parable, what do you have? You have a family: messy, passionate, sometimes self-serving and often held together only by the parents' love.

To understand the story fully, we need to take another look at its setting in Luke 15, one of the most carefully crafted chapters in the gospels. After the introductory material, setting Jesus once again at odds with those representing the tradition on matters of table fellowship, we are given a series of three stories that I think of as being parables of seeking. That is obvious in the Lost Sheep and the Lost Coin, but how is the Prodigal Son a parable of searching? I suppose the younger son was seeking fame and fortune, maybe even seeking to find himself, but that is not the seeking I have in mind.

There is an important progression and regression in the three stories, hinted at already. The shepherd takes great risk, going deeper into the wilderness to look for the stray, leaving the ninety-nine alone not only while he searches but even after he has found the sheep, as he goes home and says, "Rejoice with me." For all the risk, however, there was not that much at stake—just one sheep out of one hundred. The woman, however, has lost one tenth of her wealth, but with much more at stake she never leaves home. She loses only a little time and some oil in her lamp until she finds the drachma and says, like the shepherd, "Rejoice with me." It is the father who has the most at stake: one of his two sons is "lost . . . dead" (15:32). And what can he do? Nothing. He waits, he hopes, surely he prays. But assuming he does not know where the young man has gone, and the story does not suggest he does, the father cannot set off from one "distant country" to another and look for him. All he can do is wait, which I take to be its own kind of seeking.

The triptych of parables in Luke 15 are about seeking. Each kind of seeking is different, and something different is at stake in each one. What fascinates is the clear impression that the more there is at stake, the less there is the seeker can do about it. The shepherd takes great risk in seeking one sheep out of one hundred. At times the seeking is risky, forcing us out of ourselves in ways that we would rather not. To seek the lost, after all, means going to where they are, not waiting for them to come to us. And sometimes to find a part of our self that has been repressed or forgotten takes great psychic and spiritual risk.

But not all seeking makes such demands, even when there is much at stake. One tenth of your net worth means a lot to you, I suspect. But in the parable of the Lost Coin, the seeking was more domestic, tame—turning on a light and grabbing a broom are the kind of spiritual cleaning important to self-examination, spiritual direction, and other practices of Christian formation. In many ways we already have what we need ready to hand—it is just out of reach or out of sight. So seeking, spiritual and otherwise, is not all of a piece, one time demanding great effort, other times almost falling into our lap (think of the treasure in the field).

And then there are times, like in the story of the Lost Son, when we cannot do a thing, and those are precisely the times when the most is at stake. Surely this is often true of us as parents—from the nine months of gestation on, parenting involves much passionate waiting. From decisions we cannot make to consequences we cannot prevent, we trust that our best has been enough, we hope, we pray. But we cannot live our children's lives for them. A quick look around suggests this lesson is not limited to parents, for much of what we most passionately seek is beyond our control and in most respects entirely outside our influence—we cannot make someone love us, as much as we seek love; we cannot eliminate prejudice no matter how vigilantly we seek justice, and on and on.

That is why we need to accept waiting as its own kind of seeking. Life demands it. The Vietnamese Buddhist monk Thich Nhat Hanh has been a wonderful teacher of this truth. In books like *Peace Is Every Step*[4] he reminds us that peace is not just a goal, it is the means to its own fulfillment. Peace is not the last step; it is also the first step and every step in between. If we walk in peace, we are making peace a reality with every step, not just the last one. If we wait with patient longing, we are actively seeking, we're just not necessarily moving. This is not a call to passivity, but to recognizing that seeking comes in different guises, so the seeking we do should fit the occasion that evokes it.

Finally, when you see it, run for it. Dad's compassion sent him down the road in a rush, his waiting/seeking wonderfully rewarded. This, tragically, does not always happen when prodigals stray. But when it does, embrace with all the love in your heart and call to the rest of us, "Rejoice with me!"

Continuing the Conversation

Twenty years ago, looking for someone in Chicago to talk with about the parables, I met a wonderful conversation partner in the person of a professor at DePaul University—John Dominic Crossan. Unbeknownst to me at the time, Dom, as he is known to friends and colleagues, was at work on his masterpiece, *The Historical Jesus: The Life of a Mediterranean Jewish Peasant* (San Francisco: Harper SanFrancisco, 1993), but he was nevertheless more than happy to talk about a topic that, though I was unaware of it, had already fallen by the biblical studies wayside. You may join that conversation through his books *In Parables* (New York: Harper and Row, 1973), *Finding Is the First Act*, Semeia Supplements (Philadelphia: Fortress Press, 1979) and *The Dark Interval* (Niles, IL: Argus Communications, 1975).

CHAPTER FOUR

When the Roll Is Called Up Yonder: Parables of Judgment

Judgment. You can hear the gavel pound, the bell toll, and the theme from *Dragnet*, "dum-da-dum-dum, dum-da-dum-dum-dummm!" echoes in your ears. Judgment Day, the stuff of bad movies, guilt feelings, and the occasional nightmare.

> As I watched, thrones were set in place, and an Ancient One took his throne, his clothing was white as snow, and the hair of his head like pure wool; his throne was fiery flames, and its wheels were burning fire. A stream of fire issued and flowed out from his presence. A thousand thousands served him, and ten thousand times ten thousand stood attending him. The court sat in judgment, and the books were opened. (Dan 7:9–10)

That's what I call a judgment scene.

On the other hand, if we have faith in Christ, trust in God, and the inspiration of the Holy Spirit at work in our lives, judgment scenes may seem a little different.

> Then I saw a new heaven and a new earth; for the first heaven and the first earth had passed away, and the sea was no more. And I saw the holy city, the new Jerusalem, coming down out of heaven from God, prepared as a bride adorned for her husband. And I heard a loud voice from the

throne saying, "See, the home of God is among mortals. He will dwell with them; they will be his peoples, and God himself will be with them; he will wipe every tear from their eyes. Death will be no more; mourning and crying and pain will be no more, for the first things have passed away." (Rev 21:1–4)

Jesus told stories about both sorts of scenes, focusing on human choices and their eternal consequences. For organizational purposes I have somewhat arbitrarily divided these into parables of judgment and decision, the first group, in this chapter, emphasizing consequences (judgment) and the second group, in the next chapter, on human choices.

The Parable of the Pharisee and the Tax Collector: Gotcha!

We begin with a simple story involving two characters from Bible Central Casting and a surprising judgment from Jesus that may not be quite what we think it is.

"Two men went up to the temple to pray, one a Pharisee and the other a tax collector. The Pharisee, standing by himself, was praying thus, 'God, I thank you that I am not like other people: thieves, rogues, adulterers, or even like this tax collector. I fast twice a week; I give a tenth of all my income.' But the tax collector, standing far off, would not even look up to heaven, but was beating his breast and saying, 'God, be merciful to me, a sinner!' I tell you, this man went down to his home justified rather than the other; for all who exalt themselves will be humbled, but all who humble themselves will be exalted." (Luke 18:10–14)

What could be plainer than that—a good guy who is a bad guy and a bad guy who is a good guy, and we are supposed to be like . . . well, uh, the good guy? Maybe, but which one? The good bad guy or the bad good guy? This is not so simple after all.

A good guy who is a bad guy and a bad guy who is a good guy, and we are supposed to be like . . . well, uh, the good guy?

I think it will help to refresh our memory about the two characters. In Sunday School or Vacation Bible School we learned that tax collectors were nasty fellows who collaborated with the Romans and the Temple authorities to squeeze every last denarius and shekel from the hardworking people of Palestine, rendering unto Caesar just about everything. Tax collectors, like Zaccheus (Luke 19:1–10), were universally hated, so much so that the phrase "tax collectors and sinners" is found nine times in the gospels. Pharisees, according to our Sunday School teachers, were worse. Pious, pompous, walking around looking for something to disapprove of, hiding in cornfields to catch hungry disciples violating the Sabbath (Mark 2:23–24), opposing Jesus at every turn, their name synonymous with "hypocrite." So what we have is a story about two bad guys, one of whom is approved that is, pronounced "justified," by Jesus.

Maybe, except the version of Pharisee just outlined, while widely accepted, is deeply flawed. Instead of a pious, pompous hypocrite we need to think of someone who is faithful, committed, learned, charitable, and widely respected. The closest comparison in the Anglican Communion might be a vocational deacon. No less a luminary than the apostle Paul proudly referred to himself as a Pharisee (Phil 3:5), a member of a group that can rightly be described as a reforming movement within Judaism. Historically Pharisees were the remnant who preserved the traditions after the fall of the Temple in 70 CE, and the rabbinic movement, the Mishnah, and the Talmuds are their heritage. Further, the language in the Gospels denouncing Pharisees needs to be read carefully, lest it provide support for anti-Semitism. To be sure, the Pharisees were suspicious of Jesus as one who did not share their commitment to absolute rigor in upholding the Law as they thought it should be upheld, and to that extent they were both rivals and foils for Jesus. The rhetoric about them is often the rhetoric of dispute and argument, and should be read in that light.

As for the tax collector, let's just say that sometimes our teachers got it right in Sunday School. This was not an IRS (U.S.), HMRC (U.K.), or CRA (Canada) agent, dutifully carrying out difficult government work, under close and careful oversight. This was a collaborator, collecting taxes with military backup, more like the henchmen in a Hagar the Horrible cartoon without the humor. Tax collecting was a franchise business won at auction. Whoever promised the most taxes to the authorities got the job, and they made a profit by collecting more than what they promised to pay the Romans. How much were taxes in Jesus' day? Between the taxes due the Romans and the tithes and offerings due the Temple authorities, the tax rate was anywhere from 50 to 75 percent, and instead of being graduated, they were regressive, so that the less you earned, the higher percentage you paid. Popular fellows.

What Jesus' audience heard, then, was a story about a widely admired religious leader and a universally despised representative of the occupying authority. It was not hard to pick sides. Moreover, the prayer offered by the Pharisee was not the boastful, judgmental piece it sounds to our ears, but a version of a standard prayer of the faithful, a claiming of religious heritage and an affirmation of religious practice. As odd as it may sound to our ear, a standard prayer of the day including thanksgiving for not being a long list of things—"I thank thee, O Lord my God, that thou hast given me my lot with those who sit in the seat of learning and not with those who sit at the street-corners. . . . "[1] Are we supposed to hate the guy because he keeps, even exceeds, the requirements of his religious tradition? Jesus says, "I tell you, the tax collector was justified before God, not the Pharisee."

You could have heard a pin drop. Not that it should have been a total surprise. Jesus had already called a tax collector, Levi, to be a follower (Luke 5:27) and banqueted in his house, and soon enough he would invite himself to the house of Zaccheus (ch. 19). But still, to declare the tax collector "justified" was astounding. What is that all about? It would help if we were clear on the meaning of the term, for starters. Jesus is saying more than that the tax collector was forgiven and the Pharisee not. The Pharisee did not ask for anything and the tax collector asked for mercy; neither of them asked for forgiveness. The "mercy" the tax collector asked for is related to terms for sacrifice, so the response of being justified, made right with, is appropriate in the Temple setting of the story—you went to the Temple to offer a sacrifice to make things right with God.

In any case, both the tax collector and the Pharisee got what they asked for—the Pharisee asked for nothing and that is what he received; the tax collector asked to be made right with God and that is what Jesus says happened. On a certain level, the story acts out the teaching in the Sermon on the Mount, "Ask, and it will be given you" (Matt 7:7). You do not get what you do not ask for, the message seems to be, reinforcing the message of the parable of the Persistent Widow that immediately precedes in Luke 18. That parable, too, hints at the appropriate posture before God, in prayer and in all things.

Can it be that easy? Other than correcting a mistaken, and potentially anti-Semitic understanding of the Pharisees, it does not seem like much happened. How was the mind "teased into active thought?" It was—we just did not notice it. Recall the first question asked in this section: Which "good guy" are we supposed to be like, the good bad guy (tax collector) or the bad good guy (Pharisee)? How

To say, "I am like the Pharisee" is to say, "I stand fully sufficient before the Lord, and do not need to ask for a thing." We haven't met, but I am guessing that shoe doesn't fit.

did you answer? Take your time, because it may be a trick question. To say, "I am like the Pharisee" is to say, "I stand fully sufficient before the Lord, and do not need to ask for a thing." We haven't met, but I am guessing that shoe doesn't fit. To say, "I am like the tax collector" is to say, "I am a no-good, greedy s.o.b.," but it is also to say, "I am the one who goes home 'justified.'" That one is a little snug too, isn't it? Just like Jesus to give us a story that calls into question even our answers.

The Parable of the Unjust Judge: The Widow's Day(s) in Court

Our characters are again right out of central casting: a judge (boo! hiss!) who "neither feared God nor had respect for people" and a widow (ahh!) who has apparently been swindled or taken advantage of in some way not detailed in the parable. All that matters is that she keeps showing up in his courtroom and demanding, "Grant me justice against my opponent." Jesus shapes the story so that all the sympathy goes toward the widow, and after all, "Religion that is pure and undefiled before God, the Father, is this: to care for orphans and widows in their distress" (Jas 1:27). The story as Jesus tells it also has a bit more of an edge to it than comes through in our translations, for the judge, while admitting, "I have no fear of God and no respect for anyone" (18:4)

The judge was afraid of a thrashing from the widow, and gave her what she wanted.

decides to grant her, "justice, so that she may not wear me out by her continual coming" (18:5). The "justice" granted refers again to the justification in the parable we just considered, but the "wear me out" is at best a euphemism, for the Greek term, *hupōpiazēi*, means to beat or strike with blows, elsewhere found only in Paul, "I pommel my body" (1 Cor 9:27, RSV). So the judge was afraid of a thrashing from the widow, and gave her what she wanted.

But before we start to think of this as a cartoon or silent movie from a bygone era, we must attend to the sayings prefacing and following the story. First, Luke tells us that Jesus told the story of the persistent, pugilistic widow because of "their need to pray always and not to lose heart" (18:1). Okay, praying is like boxing, requiring training, practice, and endurance. Weird analogy, but we can work with that. But what do we do with the closing analogy?

> And the Lord said, "Listen to what the unjust judge says. And will not God grant justice to his chosen ones who cry to him day and night? Will he delay long in helping them? I tell you, he will quickly grant justice to them. And yet, when the Son of Man comes, will he find faith on earth?" (Luke 18:6–8)

It seems that Luke, if not Jesus (when the noun shifts from "Jesus" in verse 1 to "the Lord" in verse 6 we get suspicious), is comparing the unjust judge to God. Fortunately God comes off the better, not delaying and granting justice. But it is an unexpected analogy nevertheless. The analogy concludes with a disturbing rhetorical question with an eschatological (end of the age) twist about the coming of the Son of Man—will faith be found or not? Where did faith come from? I thought we were talking about prayer, patience, and judgment? Yes, the very stuff of faith.

Eschatology is the study of "end times"—*eschaton* the Greek word for "end." A passage of Scripture is "eschatological" if it makes reference to or describes what the "end times" will be like.

I have included these two parables from Luke 18 in this chapter on judgment because sometimes the judgment is in our favor. Jesus, the unjust judge, and God grant and pronounce justice, or righteousness, announcing or establishing right-relationship with God. But the judgment can also go against us. We will look at one example from Luke before turning to five stories in Matthew.

The Rich Man and Lazarus: Smoking or Non-Smoking

The rabbis told the story of two men, a poor scholar and a wealthy merchant, who died on the same day. The merchant was buried with little heed, but the scholar was sent off in style, honored by the community in death as he never had been in life. This reversal, articulated by Jesus as "the last will be first and the first will be last" (Matt

20:16) and by James as, "Let the believer who is lowly boast in being raised up, and the rich in being brought low" (1:9–10), is fairly standard stuff in our tradition. Most New Testament scholars take the story of the rich man and the poor beggar to be a part of the same folklore tradition as the story told by the rabbis.

> "There was a rich man who was dressed in purple and fine linen and who feasted sumptuously every day. And at his gate lay a poor man named Lazarus, covered with sores, who longed to satisfy his hunger with what fell from the rich man's table; even the dogs would come and lick his sores. The poor man died and was carried away by the angels to be with Abraham. The rich man also died and was buried. In Hades, where he was being tormented, he looked up and saw Abraham far away with Lazarus by his side. He called out, 'Father Abraham, have mercy on me, and send Lazarus to dip the tip of his finger in water and cool my tongue; for I am in agony in these flames.' But Abraham said, 'Child, remember that during your lifetime you received your good things, and Lazarus in like manner evil things; but now he is comforted here, and you are in agony. Besides all this, between you and us a great chasm has been fixed, so that those who might want to pass from here to you cannot do so, and no one can cross from there to us.' He said, 'Then, father, I beg you to send him to my father's house—for I have five brothers—that he may warn them, so that they will not also come into this place of torment.' Abraham replied, 'They have Moses and the prophets; they should listen to them.' He said, 'No, father Abraham; but if someone goes to them from the dead, they will repent.' He said to him, 'If they do not listen to Moses and the prophets, neither will they be convinced even if someone rises from the dead.'" (Luke 16:19–31)

The story is in three scenes. First we meet the rich man (who is not named) and the poor beggar, their respective conditions vividly described. In the second scene they die, and their fate in the hereafter is described even more strikingly, Lazarus rocking his soul in the bosom of Abraham and the rich man in a world of everlasting hurt. The third and longest scene details the rich man's hope for a little relief, and then, in perhaps the first unselfish request of his life, that Lazarus be sent to his brothers to warn them that they should pay attention to what their momma taught about heaven and heck. Abraham had to say no. It is quite a story, and we should begin by reminding ourselves that it is a story, filled with folkloric detail, not Jesus' description of heaven and hell. Next, note the two fundamental principles driving the narrative—the principle of reversal and the "great chasm" between Hades and heaven that cannot be crossed.

The idea of reversal—last/first, the poor, hungry, grieving, persecuted "blessed" (Matt 5:3–12), the dead raised—so central to Christian truth is here vividly, almost shockingly, depicted. What, after all, did the rich man do? We are not told that he was unjust like the judge, or that he murdered, cheated on his spouse, or kicked his dog. Only that he dressed and ate well. Is that a crime? (Actually it may be, or it may have been sufficient evidence of possible wrongdoing in that culture to convict, but we will look at attitudes about wealth in the next chapter.)

What we do know is what the rich man did *not* do. Maybe, at least, he should have given his dogs a shove so that they did not lick Lazarus' sores. Maybe he should have allowed Lazarus the table scraps. He knew Lazarus well enough to call him by name when talking to Abraham, if only to request an act of service for himself and his brothers. Did he not know him enough to care for him, to "love his neighbor" as himself (Lev 19:18) and "open his hand to the poor and needy" (Deut 15:11), as the Law and the Prophets taught?

And then there is the chasm, and what happens on the wrong side of it. Summer church camp preachers have long used the closing bonfire as an occasion to mix metaphors with abandon, first depicting the warmth and brightness of God's love and then the fiery torments of heck. Thirty years ago, the satirical Evangelical magazine *The Wittenburg Door* celebrated as the "Loser of the Month" an evangelist who set his shirt on fire at the climax of his message warning about the fiery finish awaiting those who did not repent (I am not making this up). From the burning fiery furnace in the Book of Daniel to cartoons in *The New Yorker*, the fires of hell are well attested. On the good side, in our story and in movies like *It's a Wonderful Life*, cartoons with puffy clouds, and jokes about one group or another sitting by themselves because they think they are the only ones in heaven, there are all sorts of popular images of the hereafter.

Bad preaching and joking aside, something serious is going on in this story of judgment. It's saying that our eternity is decided by our present choices. While Lazarus could not cross into Hades, the reason he is not sent to Earth to warn the rich man's brothers is not that he could not, but that it would do no good. The brothers had all the information they needed. They knew what to do and what God expected of them. So do we. The story reminds us of the consequences of what we choose to do with what we already know.

Ouch. I know, it is only a story, but must judgment be so harsh? In fact, it can be a good bit harsher when Matthew gets his hands on it.

The Unforgiving Servant: Use It or Lose It

The parable of the Unforgiving Servant is long, but can be simply retold. Based on the numbers involved (10,000 talents is Bill Gates kind of money), Jesus appears to want us to think of a king and two provincial rulers. The king orders an audit and finds that one of the men owes him a bundle. He was embezzling or cheating in one form or another, and the king orders him (and his family—that's the way they did things back then) tossed into prison. But the man begged, "Have patience with me, and I will pay you everything" (Matt 18:26). Miracle of miracles, the king did have patience. So the servant waltzes out and bumps into the next guy in line, who happens to owe *him* a not insignificant sum, but nevertheless around 100,000 times less than the debt he himself had just had forgiven. And what does he say? "Hey, that 100 denarii you owe me? Fuhgettaboutit!" Not on your life. He grabs the second man by the throat and demands instant repayment, in cash—no checks, no credit cards. Fighting for air, the other fellow says, "Have patience with me, and I will pay you" (18:29, almost word for word the same thing the first man said to the king). But the first man refuses and has the second man jailed, which infuriates those looking on, who report the incident to the king. You can imagine how that goes over. "You wicked slave! I forgave you all that debt because you pleaded with me. Should you not have had mercy on your fellow slave, as I had mercy on you?" (18:32–33). And he tosses him into prison for keeps (how Matthew avoided mentioning the weeping and gnashing of teeth is a mystery).

As noted, the details of the story—the amounts involved and the tossing into prison in particular—suggest a story of the king and his

10,000 talents is Bill Gates kind of money.

court. Ten thousand talents, *myriad talentos* in Greek, is the largest number that can be easily expressed in the Koine Greek of the New Testament, larger numbers being multiples of *myriad* (cf. Rev 5:11). So there is little point in calculating what the amount might be except to highlight the difference in the debts owed by the two servants. We start with the denarius, which is, based on the parable to follow, reckoned as one day's wage, at minimum wage. One hundred denarii is significant, but certainly repayable. Ten thousand talents, however, is another matter altogether, for a talent is usually reckoned as around 4,500 to 5,000 denarii, or fifteen years of work at minimum wage. Do the math and you realize that the debt is 150,000 years of work for the daily worker, or as I said, Bill Gates kind of cash. A debt, in other words, that could never be repaid. But it was. "And out of pity for him, the lord of that slave released him and forgave him the debt" (Matt 18:27).

If you have ever owed someone something you had no idea how you would ever repay, you have some sense of how good it must have felt to the servant, not to mention the family, to have the debt forgiven. But how long did that good feeling last—ten seconds? Or was the servant the sort who never made a connection between how he wanted to be treated and how he treated others? Either way, he wanted his hundred denarii, no matter the cost to his colleague. The result of his inability to learn from his own experience, of his greed, or simply of the kind of jerk he really was, crashed down on him soon enough. He was not just tossed in prison, he was "handed over to be tortured" (18:34).

It is okay to get all Jesus-y here. The unpayable debt, the language of lord, king, and slaves, the hellish alternative to the debt being paid point clearly in that direction. As does the language of verse 27 quoted already, "out of *pity* for him." We saw the word translated as *pity* in the last chapter to describe the feeling of the prodigal's father (Luke 15:20), where it was better translated as "filled with compassion." Pity no longer communicates what Scripture means. A lord who has compassion on a servant with a debt that cannot be repaid forgives the debt.

As sweet and wonderful as this is, however, it is not the focus of the parable. If it were the focus, it would be an allegory. The focus, instead, is on the actions and attitudes of the first servant. He could not learn. It is not hard to imagine the huge debt not being the first time he had run into trouble, nor the first time he managed to sweet-talk his way out of trouble. All he had to do was "go and do likewise" (Luke 10:37) and he would have been off free and easy. But he could-n't do it. He couldn't walk away. He couldn't learn from what he had just experienced. After all, that was his money he was owed. He only wanted justice.

There is a traditional reading of the story that focuses on the justice of being handed over to the torturers; in this reading, God is the King and the slaves are the miserable wretches dangling in God's angry hand. Yuck. This parable of judgment can be read in that way, but it distracts us from the emphasis of the story itself on the absolute necessity of learning from our experience, of learning from God's grace. How often we go through life expecting others to appreciate our special circumstances, to recognize that "after all, I meant well," and all the other justifications we find for our own (mis)behavior. But let someone do something to us, forget a commitment they made, and so on, and we are like the most unforgiving lion in the jungle.

What's the maxim? What goes around comes around. Do you want that to be grace and forgiveness in your life? Me too.

The Laborers in the Vineyard: Is Fair, Fair?

Another long parable in Matthew is easily summarized. It is harvest time at the vineyard, and the owner goes to the local Manpower office—the nearest corner, in his case—and hires those looking for work at 6 AM. They agree on the going rate—a denarius for the day (probably with lunch included). He takes his pickup back by the corner at 9 AM and rounds up some more, promising only to give them what is fair, and does the same at noon and at three o'clock. With darkness closing in and the work almost done, he drives past the corner one more time and hires the late risers. At quitting time, he follows the Torah ("you shall not keep for yourself the wages of a laborer until morning," Lev 19:13) and pays everyone, beginning with the late sleepers hired at 5 PM. To their delight, he pays them a denarius—a day's pay for an hour's work. Everyone looking on fig-ures they are in for a fabulous payday, but they all get a denarius apiece. You can hear the grumbling across the millennia: "It's not fair!" But the owner is not impressed: "Friend, I am doing you no wrong; did you not agree with me for the usual daily wage? Take what belongs to you and go; I choose to give to this last the same as I give to you. Am I not allowed to do what I choose with what belongs to me? Or are you envious because I am generous?" (Matt 20:13–15).

I don't care what the vineyard owner says—it is *not* fair. What do you think will happen the next time he looks for workers at 6 AM? Who will go out to work all day, and in the heat of the day at that (v. 12), in his fields? No one. Would you? And, since Matthew tells us that Jesus begins the story, "The kingdom of heaven is like . . ." we are supposed to make some comparison between the vineyard owner, workers, their pay, and life in the kingdom. Any guesses?

I told a slightly updated version of the story to my teenage daughter and she said, "The owner is an @#$." Then I pointed out that Jesus intended us to learn something about the kingdom of heaven and she said, "Well, then, who would want to live there?" She has a point. I can think of no code or standard of just behavior that advocates paying workers so cavalierly. I have heard many explanations, such as the fact that a denarius a day would barely feed a family, and if the owner paid less he would put families at risk. But that is such a contemporary response to an ancient story it scarcely merits mention. That is being nice, not living in the kingdom.

The oddest phrase in the whole story may provide a clue. It is the last one, poorly translated in the NRSV as a rhyme, "Or are you envious because I am generous?" The Greek, *hē ho opthalmos sou ponēros hoti egō agathos eimi*, means, literally, "Or is your eye evil because I am good?" which conjures up a slightly different meaning world, with evil eyes and a claim by the vineyard owner to be "good." An evil eye cannot see anything good. That world of meaning also calls to mind Jesus' response to the rich young man, "Why do you ask me about what is good? There is only one who is good" (Matt 19:17) in the passage immediately preceding our parable. Or as Mark phrases it, "No one is good but God alone" (10:18). And, it seems, the owner of the vineyard.

The parable of the Laborers in the Vineyard is not about judgment or justice. It is about goodness. Payment is made not on what is deserved, nor even on what is needed, but on what the *One* who is good gives. James puts it in his own wonderfully curious fashion, "Every generous (Gk. *agathē*, good) act of giving, with every perfect gift, is from above, coming down from the

The parable of the laborers in the vineyard is not about judgment or justice. It is about goodness.

Father of lights, with whom there is no variation or shadow due to change" (Jas 1:17). My and my daughter's senses of fair play are absolutely violated, because even when thinking about God's kingdom, we apply human standards. The harder you work, the more you get. Only those who have suffered and served for a lifetime deserve to enjoy the goodness of God's kingdom. One-hour workers don't belong any more than deathbed converts, and if God insists on letting them in, they at least should not have seats as good as ours! Put them on one of the clouds in the back, far from the harps and the heavenly banquet.

But there they are, not only sitting in the front row sipping something cool and frosty, but they GOT THERE FIRST!

It isn't fair.

Just good.

The Stories of Matt 25:
What Have You Done For Me, Lately?

Matthew, Mark, and Luke are referred to as the "Synoptic Gospels" because they follow the same basic outline, or synopsis, in their presentation of Jesus' life, death, and resurrection; Mark is believed to have been written first, with Matthew and Luke following along in the same pattern. John does his own thing. He includes no parables in his gospel, and does not figure in this study. But the first three Evangelists don't move in lockstep, and in the chapter before us Matthew does something unique, inserting three stories about judgment between Jesus' discourse about the end of the age and the passion narrative proper.

The three long narratives that make up Matt 25 are well known, and illustrate to some scholars three different genres—allegory (the Ten Maidens), parable (the Talents), and example story (the Sheep and Goats), though, as with most matters, scholars often do not agree on those distinctions. At the risk of confusing one and all, I want to look at the stories together, but in a slightly different order, beginning with the Talents, then the Maidens, and concluding with the judgment scene described in the narrative at the end of the chapter, the Sheep and Goats.

THE PARABLE OF THE TALENTS

This parable is found in a much different version in Luke 19:11–27, where the talents are downsized to pounds (Gk. *mnas*, worth approximately 100 denarii), the servants increased to ten, and the person handing out the cash is a king, all of which we will now ignore in our focus on Matt 25. Most Christians, Anglican and otherwise, hear an annual homiletic reference during "stewardship season" about the three servants entrusted with differing sums by their master before he travels—one, two, and five talents, with talent as sum of money quickly morphing into talent as ability or skill and concluding with an admonition to give generously of our time, talent, and treasure. The story itself is about something else altogether. Two of the servants prove to be risk-taking, self-starting entrepreneurial types, doubling the money entrusted to them seemingly overnight. The third servant reminds us of the sort of fellow who must have buried the treasure in Matt 13:44 and forgot to tell his heirs about it, leaving it for a lucky stranger to find, except this one digs it up and hands it back to his master.

We are not told how the first two managed to invest so successfully because it does not matter. It is the contrast between their risk and the third servant's fear, and the response of the master, that drives the story. The first two are, of course, rewarded. "Well done, good and trustworthy slave, you have been trustworthy in a few things, I will put you in charge of many things, enter into the joy of your master" (Matt 25:21, 23). Servant number three fares much worse, returning the one talent with relief and saying, "Master, I knew that you were a harsh man, reaping where you did not sow, and gathering where you did not scatter seed; so I was afraid, and I went and hid your talent in the ground. Here you have what is yours" (Matt 25:24–25). The master was furious. "You wicked and lazy slave! You knew, did you, that I reap where I did not sow, and gather where I did not scatter? Then you ought to have invested my money with the bankers, and on my return I would have received what was my own with interest" (25:26–27). Then he takes the talent from him, gives it to the first servant, and Matthew being Matthew, orders "this worthless slave" to be cast "into the outer darkness, where there will be weeping and gnashing of teeth" (25:30). It seems we need to pay attention to what we are doing with what we've got.

THE STORY OF THE TEN MAIDENS

Matthew 25:1–13 starts with a bachelor party that lasts too long and ends with a door slammed in the face and locked tight. The NRSV calls our heroines "bridesmaids," but the Greek is *parthenois*, virgins. We know almost nothing about first-century Jewish wedding customs, but the virgins' role seems to involve accompanying the bridegroom in procession to the wedding celebration, with their lamps ablaze. For whatever reason the groom is late, and the maidens *all* fall asleep. At midnight the guy finally shows and the drowsy maidens rush to meet him. Five of them

> The story of the Ten Maidens starts with a bachelor party that lasts too long and ends with a door slammed in the face and locked tight.

discover to their horror that they did not bring enough oil and their lamps will not light. They ask to borrow some oil from the others, who claim they do not have enough for everyone and then send the "foolish" five off to Wal-Mart to buy some. It takes a while to find the all-night oil emporium, and by the time the five maidens return, the procession is over and the wedding celebration has begun; the door is locked and the velvet rope is manned to prevent wedding crashers. "Lord, lord, open to us" they beg, but it is too late. "Truly I tell you, I do not know you." Matthew adds a saying similar to one found at the end of Chapter 24 about not knowing the day or hour, and admonishes all to "stay awake," which, while it fits Mark 13:35–37 and parallels (the sleeping servants), makes no sense in this story, for all the maidens—those with oil and those without—fall asleep. It does, however, give rise to the wonderful sermonic non sequitur known to awaken even teenage boys in the back pew, "And so I ask you, do you want to stay awake and watch with the wise maidens, or sleep with the foolish virgins?" In any case, it seems that not only does it matter what we do with what we have, but how well prepared we are to do what is expected of us when the moment for action arrives.

THE SHEEP AND THE GOATS

Finally, and I do mean finally, Matt 25:31–46. It is not a parable, nor an allegory, but an in-between genre short on narrative and long on impact. The scene is set at the end of the age: "When the Son of Man comes in his glory, and all the angels with him, then he will sit on the throne of his glory" (25:31). Then the people are separated "as a shepherd separates the sheep from the goats. To those on the right he says, 'Come, you that are blessed by my Father'" (25:34) and to those on the left, "You that are accursed, depart from me into the eternal fire prepared for the devil and his angels" (25:41). What is the basis of this overwhelming and absolute judgment? Simple:

- I was hungry and you gave me food or gave me no food.
- I was thirsty and you gave me something to drink or nothing to drink.
- I was a stranger and you welcomed me or did not welcome me.
- I was naked and you gave me clothing or did not give me clothing.
- I was sick and in prison and you cared for and visited me or did not care for nor visit me.

When did they do or not do this? Also simple: "Truly I tell you, just as you did—or did not do it—to one of the least of those who are members of my family, you did it—or did it not—to me" (25:40, 45). It seems it matters greatly what we do even when we think no one we know is looking.

Matthew used a distinctive strategy in constructing his gospel, fashioning five "sermons" (chs. 5–7, the Sermon on the Mount, ch. 10 on missionary discipleship, ch. 13 on the parables, ch. 18 on community discipline) ending in chapters 24 through 25 on the end of the age. Over the years we have learned to read these sermons as rhetorical units, but rarely is this reading strategy applied to Matt 25. Instead, we isolate each parable and read it without regard to its context in Matthew's shaping of Jesus' sermon on the judgment at the end of the age. The loss is ours.

The three stories in chapter 25 are about the consequences of actions, or, more often, inaction. The foolish maidens not only could not light their lamps; they failed to join the bridal procession in a ridiculous midnight search for oil. The third servant in the parable of the Talents buried his master's money, and perhaps sat on it like a brooding hen, not even depositing the funds at his local branch bank to earn interest (and a free toaster!). The "goats" in the third narrative saw human need, but failing to recognize in whose image the needy were created did nothing to relieve that need. James spectacularly captures this failure in a saying that sounds a lot like Jesus. "What good is it, my brothers and sisters, if you say you have faith but do not have works? Can faith save you? If a brother or sister is naked and lacks daily food, and one of you says to them, 'Go in peace; keep warm and eat your fill,' and yet you do not supply their bodily needs, what is the good of that?" (Jas 2:14–16).

What is the good of that? Great question. The cumulative force of the three narratives is that the Book of Life opened on Judgment Day will not be turned to an opinion survey but an inventory of our actions. At the Pearly Gates, St. Peter is not going to ask after our Christology but our Christ-likeness; not whether we agree with Paul that "we know a person is justified not by works of the law but through faith in Jesus Christ" (Gal 2:16), but whether we lived as if "faith by itself, if it has no works, is dead" (Jas 2:17).

Now matters become tricky, for the issue is much like that of the unforgiving servant. What are we going to do with what we know? How will we use the grace we have been given? The temptation to use our understanding of the standards to be applied on Judgment Day in helping us evaluate others is formidable. It's important, isn't it, to point out to others their many faults and failings lest they wind up on the wrong side of the chasm? Important, but it is not our job. We are to take what we have learned about the real final exam and use it personally, judging ourselves in light of the parables of judgment we've just studied.

How you doing?

Continuing the Conversation

Did Jesus "invent" parable? No, not rhetorically. Aristotle writes of them hundreds of years before Jesus is born. However, in its full narrative form there is nothing in the Hebrew Bible or other ancient literatures exactly like the stories of Jesus we call parables, just as there is nothing quite like "gospel" until the Gospel of Mark. This is not to say, however, that Jesus' storytelling was detached from its antecedents in Hebrew Scripture, nor from its cousins in the literature of the rabbis. The parallels are interesting, and well worth study. Three books that help us study the parallels between Jesus and the rabbis are *Parable and Story in Judaism and Christianity*, edited by Thoma and Wyschorod (New York: Paulist Press, 1989), *Jesus and His Jewish Parables* by Brad Young (New York: Paulist Press, 1989), and *They Also Taught in Parables: Rabbinic Parables from the First Centuries of the Christian Era*, collected by McArthur and Johnson (Grand Rapids: Zondervan, 1990).

CHAPTER FIVE

I Have Decided to Follow Jesus: Parables of Decision

The difference between parables of judgment and parables of decision may be in the eye of the interpreter. Nevertheless, I think an important distinction can be made, and not just for the sake of balanced chapter divisions in books like this. In the parables and stories considered in the previous chapter, the narrative focus was on what happened after a decision was made by a leading protagonist or group of protagonists: the decision by the vineyard owner to pay everyone the same and the conversation that ensues; Abraham speaking to the rich man in Hades; the judgment of the master after the one-talent servant chose to bury the money rather than invest it; the locked door facing the foolish maidens, and so on. In this chapter we'll see that the focus is more on the deliberation and decision of the protagonists themselves. The judgment, while not merely an afterthought, is of secondary importance. Interestingly, while most of the parables in the last chapter were from Matthew, with the exception of the brief story with which we begin all the parables in this chapter are from Luke. You can draw your own conclusion about that.

The Two Sons: Talk Is Cheap

"What do you think? A man had two sons; he went to the first and said, 'Son, go and work in the vineyard today.' He answered, 'I will not'; but later he changed his mind and went. The father went to the second and said the same; and he answered, 'I go, sir'; but he did not go. Which of the two did the will of his father?" They said, "The first." Jesus said to them, "Truly I tell you, the tax collectors and the prostitutes are going into the kingdom of God ahead of you." (Matthew 21:28–31)

Kids. We only have one, but she is perfectly capable of acting like the two sons in this story in any given hour. Clearly this family is "drawn from nature or common life." Which is not to say they lived next door to Jesus any more than the prodigal father and his two sons did. It is to say that Jesus describes a familiar experience or reality and relates it to God's kingdom and reign. Except for the part about tax collectors and prostitutes. Where did that come from?

Same place, the common life, or have you not noticed that our towns also have those who are treated like second- (or no-) class citizens? Matthew's context is important, because this story is told on what we think of as the first day of Holy Week. They've swept up after the parade on "Palm Sunday" and straightened up the money-changing tables. The fig tree has been cursed and withered, Jesus is teaching away in the Temple, and the "chief priests and elders of the people" (Matt 21:23) want to know just who Jesus thinks he is. He says he'll tell them, if they first tell him who they think John the Baptist was. They won't, so Jesus doesn't.

Then he tells them about the two sons. The first child is honest. "No way, I don't want to! Why do I have to do everything around here? You've ruined my life!" A little later, with nothing good on television and all his buddies at camp, he decides he might as well go to the vineyard and help out. The second child responds respectfully, "I go, sir." Sir? The Greek term, *kyrios*, can also be translated as "lord." What a suck-up. But what does he do? Nothing. And as long as I am playing with Greek, it is worth noting that the word used to describe the first son's change of heart, *metamelomai*, can mean "regret" and even "repent."

> The first child is honest. "No way, I don't want to! Why do I have to do everything around here? You've ruined my life!"

The contrast is between words and deeds, with a change of mind, if not heart, between one and the other. The question asked, "Which of the two *did* the will of his father?" answers itself because only one of the two *did* anything. At this point I can imagine Jesus' audience nodding in approval. No grandstanding and showboating for them. They aren't like those who want to *look* like they are doing God's will; they are the ones who actually do it. Hey, maybe this Jesus isn't so bad after all.

"Truly I tell you, the tax collectors and the prostitutes are going into the kingdom of God ahead of you." What! That's outrageous! Maybe prophets and priest get to go in before us, but greedy traitors and harlots? This Jesus fellow is worse than we heard. Somebody's got to do something.

Exactly. Do something. We saw at the end of the last chapter that Judgment Day is not going to involve SAT scores and résumés, but showing the dirt under our fingernails. As we move into deeper consideration of four parables of decision, we are reminded that the decision is about our actions, not our words.

The Two Towers and the King: Planned Obsolescence

You get the new purchase home, plug it in, and enjoy it for a while. Three days after the warranty expires, it breaks. You think, well, I really liked this thing, maybe I'll have it fixed. Trouble is they don't make the parts any more. It happens all the time, with everything from tennis shoes to televisions. Does it also happen to faith?

> "For which of you, intending to build a tower, does not first sit down and estimate the cost, to see whether he has enough to complete it? Otherwise, when he has laid a foundation and is not able to finish, all who see it will begin to ridicule him, saying, 'This fellow began to build and was not able to finish.' Or what king, going out to wage war against another king, will not sit down first and consider whether he is able with ten thousand to oppose the one who comes against him with twenty thousand? If he cannot, then, while the other is still far away, he sends a delegation and asks for the terms of peace." (Luke 14:28–32)

The nature or common life thing may be a stretch here. Most of us with building plans are thinking about an addition to our house, not a tower for our castle, and kings deciding whether to go to war are largely relegated to history books. However, all of us make decisions all of the time, and the intriguing aspect of this passage—indeed the whole of Luke 14—is that Jesus treats the life of faith as a matter for deliberate decision, and not as a spiritual response to a moment of inspiration.

The shorthand for this is, "Can you finish what you start?" That is a common question, and one we apply to many aspects of life, from telling kids to "take all you want but eat all you take" to enrolling in graduate school, accepting a vestry position, and planning for retirement. What is odd ("arrests the hearer by its vividness or strangeness") is to include the life of faith in such a series of calculations. Paul did not pause after being blinded by the light on the road to Damascus and deliberate about his response to the call of Christ (Acts 9), Luther didn't wonder whether to submit the ninety-five theses to a peer-reviewed journal, and Wesley didn't ask if his heart was strangely warmed by that night's dinner or by the Holy Spirit. They didn't dilly-dally—they charged forth in the name of Christ. So what's all this about counting the cost?

First, notice that Jesus is indeed not talking about anything simple or mundane, but the stuff of kings and generals. This is not about how much to put on our plates, but about building a skyscraper. Going to graduate or professional school is an important decision, but Jesus is talking about facing 20,000 hostile troops. So the figurative stakes are high. Second, the presumption is that the stakes are so high as to be insurmountable. The tower will cost too much, the foe is too formidable. So what do you do? Build a lean-to and sue for peace, or people will laugh and the enemy will defeat you. Better to settle for something less impressive than a tower, or for a negotiated peace, than to risk failure and defeat. The picture painted in the parables is not pretty. It is about difficult, almost impossible choices. And this is supposed to be in some measure about life in the kingdom of God?

Violating (again) my intention not to worry much about the context of the parables in the gospels, and knowing that careful readers have already noticed the verses surrounding the twin parables about counting the cost, I concede that here, as in many of the parables of decision, context is important for interpretation. After a transitional verse away from the parable of the Banquet, which we will look at soon, Luke relates one of the single most difficult sayings attributed to Jesus in Scripture, "Whoever comes to me and does not hate father and mother, wife and children, brothers and sisters, yes, and even life itself, cannot be my disciple" (Luke 14:26), and follows it up with the equally challenging, "Whoever does not carry the cross and follow me cannot be my disciple" (14:27). After the parable comes my favorite verse to explore with those who insist the Bible must be read literally, "So therefore, none of you can become my disciple if you do not give up all your possessions" (14:33—to which I usually add, "Can I have the keys to your Lexus?").

Synecdoche is a figure of speech using a part to represent the whole, "sail" for "ship" or "cross" for the passion of Christ and for the believer's life of faith.

These three sayings are as ripe with metaphor, hyperbole, synecdoche (using the part to represent the whole, in this case the "cross" for the life of faith) as any parable in the gospels. To read them literally means our only possession is a cross, our only feeling self-loathing, and our response to those we are taught to honor and cherish is hatred. Because that literally makes no sense, how do we make sense of it? As Jesus' way of vividly (and I suppose Dodd is right again, "strangely") teaching us that the life of discipleship is costly indeed.

The twentieth-century German theologian and martyr Dietrich Bonhoeffer famously made this point in his commentary on the Sermon on the Mount titled in English, *The Cost of Discipleship*, by distinguishing "cheap grace" from "costly grace."[1] Cheap grace is bought and sold in the marketplace so that the church is always in danger of becoming like "cheapjack wares" sold by a peddler at a flea market. It is "grace without cost" to anyone, as easily acquired as it is forgotten, such as the seed sown on rocky or thorny ground in the Allegory of the Seed and Soils (Mark 4:16–19). But that is in fact no grace, for the grace of Jesus Christ is costly, costing nothing less than the life of Jesus, and costing the believer his or her own life ("When Christ calls a man, he bid him come and die," wrote Bonhoeffer[2]). Neither Jesus nor the church would have us understand it any other way. In the parables and the sayings that surround them, Jesus is telling us of the cost because he wants us to know what we are getting into before we say, "Yes, Lord."

To return to tower-building and battle-planning, the heart of the comparison is saying that the life of faith requires that we "first sit down and estimate the cost" (Luke 14:28). It remains an odd image for the life of faith, intended to "tease our mind into active thought." What do you think? I think it is the truth for many of us. We are more like the philosopher Pascal, wagering that believing in God is more reasonable than not believing, than we are like Luther, standing firm because we "can do no other." Many of us can imagine a lot of things, entertain a variety of possibilities, and have seen the lived results of different choices, yet we *choose* faith because faith makes more sense than not, and because a life of faith is more attractive and meaningful than a life without it. Not everyone comes to faith by way of a once-for-all, life-changing, heart-warming encounter with the Divine. This does not mean that we don't like to sing "Amazing Grace" and "Just as I Am," or have a place in our theology for conversion (*metanoia*) or repentance (*metamelomai*), but that there is more than one way to come to faith. Nevertheless, faith as a "calculation" seems a little cold, so what was Jesus getting at?

Looking around us, and looking back on how the gospel has been represented and misrepresented over the centuries, we might say that Jesus is giving us a warning against over-simplifying or sugarcoating the demands of the gospel. "Just as I Am," after all, is where we start, not where Jesus wants us to end up, and getting "from where we are to where under Christ we are called to be" (to use my late father's favorite description of discipleship) can be a long and challenging journey. Since Jesus also warns us not to look back or plan for delays once we get started on that journey (Luke 9:59–62), it is better to make our calculations beforehand.

The Rich Fool:
He Who Dies with the Most Toys Is Still Dead

> Then he told them a parable: "The land of a rich man produced abundantly. And he thought to himself, 'What should I do, for I have no place to store my crops?' Then he said, 'I will do this: I will pull down my barns and build larger ones, and there I will store all my grain and my goods. And I will say to my soul, "Soul, you have ample goods laid up for many years; relax, eat, drink, be merry."' But God said to him, 'You fool! This very night your life is being demanded of you. And the things you have prepared, whose will they be?' So it is with those who store up treasures for themselves but are not rich toward God." (Luke 12:16–21)

Did Jesus hate rich people? After all, in Luke he says, "Blessed are you who are poor . . . but woe to you who are rich" (6:20, 24). Of course he also hung out with Simon the wealthy leper and Zaccheus the rich tax collector (Luke 5, 19). Yes, he required them to make some changes, but surely he did not hate them. Jesus looked on the one with many possessions, Mark says, and "loved him" (Mark 10:21), so he did not hate all rich people. He could sure be hard on them, though. Just look at the guy in the story from Luke 12. What did the guy do to deserve such a terrible fate? Nothing, if you ask me. We'll consider first-century presumptions on matters of wealth and property when we look at the next parable. Right now the details and dynamic of the parable of the "rich fool" are well worth considering in full.

A wealthy farmer has a very good year, a bumper crop in fact, producing more grain than his barns can hold, so he has a decision to make. "What should I do, for I have no place to store my crops?" What are the options? He could store the excess grain in a neighbor's barn, but that would involve the expense of hauling the grain and paying the neighbor for storage. He could leave the excess in the field for the gleaners (Lev 19:9—close by "you shall love your neighbor as yourself" in 19:18), but that is no way to get ahead. Might as well just harvest the grain and give it away to the poor, as if that is any way to run a business. He could build an extra barn, but to do so would mean either taking good land out of production or paving over the swimming pool. Tough choices. Then it comes to him, "I will do this: I will pull down my barns and build larger ones, and there I will store all my grain and my goods" (Luke 12:18). A perfect plan—no waste, no want, with some extra storage space for his vintage Mustang that really ought to be out from under the sun.

He kicks back, watches the workers dismantle and rebuild his barns, and recalls a favorite passage of Scripture: "So I commend enjoyment, for there is nothing better for people under the sun than to eat, and drink, and enjoy themselves, for this will go with them in their toil through the days of life that God gives them under the sun" (Eccl 8:15). Admittedly, like a lot of us do when quoting Scripture, he leaves some things out and rephrases a couple of other things, but his version, "Soul, you have ample goods laid up for many years; relax, eat, drink, be merry," while sounding more like the first half of Sir 11:19 than Ecclesiastes, gets the point.

In summary, a rich man does what the rich do—he got richer, not through any apparent dishonesty, graft, or exploitation, but through the good fortune of a bumper crop. He makes a prudent business decision enabling him to maximize the advantage of his good fortune, and then quotes Scripture. To which God says, "You fool!"

> A rich man does what the rich do, he got richer, not through any apparent dishonesty, graft, or exploitation, but through the good fortune of a bumper crop.

Whoa, slow down here. Am I missing something, or did God just call this fellow a name Jesus warns us not to use in the Sermon on the Mount ("and if you say, 'You fool,' you will be liable to the hell of fire" [Matthew 5:22]—the Greek terms, *aphrōn* in Luke and *mōre* in Matthew are synonyms). Is this a double standard?

Of course it is—God's standards are a little different than ours, don't you think? More to the point, "fool" is a category in the biblical lexicon, and is here used to link the decision of the rich farmer to the "fools" who in the Wisdom Tradition prominent in Psalms, Proverbs, and elsewhere "say in their heart, 'There is no God'" (Psalm 14:1). That is a link for God to make. What makes the man foolish is not what he did and said, but the attitude that was at the root of his decision-making process. He decided as one who lived only for himself and thought that he would live indefinitely. It was not some terrible punishment that befell the farmer, it was life. And death.

> Let the believer who is lowly boast in being raised up, and the rich in being brought low, because the rich will disappear like a flower in the field. For the sun rises with its scorching heat and withers the field; its flower falls, and its beauty perishes. It is the same way with the rich; in the midst of a busy life, they will wither away. (Jas 1:9–11)

James here expresses a Wisdom Tradition apparently unknown to the rich farmer but very familiar to Jesus, James' brother. The principle of reversal was discussed in the last chapter as we looked at the story of another rich man and the poor man at his gate, Lazarus. James and Jesus are here saying something a little different. It is not that rich people will die and poor people will not; it is that rich people sometimes have a way of living as if they think they will never die. But they will, and if they wait until then to discover that "life does not consist in the abundance of possessions" (Luke 12:15), it will be too late in all kinds of ways.

Our rich farmer was right to think that opportunity was knocking when rain and snow watered the earth just right (Isa 55:10), when the sun shone down on his fields whether he was righteous or not (Matt 5:45), and his land yielded grain in abundance (Psalm 72:16). But it was not an opportunity to line his pockets with another layer or two, it was an opportunity to become "rich toward God." Not because "this very night your life is being demanded of you. And the things you have prepared, whose will they be?" (Luke 12:20). But because there comes such a night in everyone's life, rich or poor.

All sorts of thoughts come from reading this story, but let's focus on three. First, this story is about you and me, and not just because I have seen the cars in your garage (or if you are like lots of folks, in your driveway because your garage is so crammed full of stuff your cars don't fit). You are rich because you could afford this book (and we thank you). I know, I know, no one in the United States is rich. Even Bill Gates is just comfortably well off, at least based on his wardrobe. But we all know that is a lie, whether we make global or merely local comparisons. So let's not pretend that the question, "Does Jesus hate rich people?" lacks personal interest.

Second, the story forces us to ask ourselves what our definition of "enough" is. The "masters of the universe" on Wall Street used to speculate on what their "number" was: how much did they "need" before they would have enough to live as they wished for the rest of their lives? When I first read about such discussions, the number had already jumped from ten to fifty million dollars, but fifty million only goes so far, and what with the price of gasoline and Gulfstream jets going up, the last mention of the topic I saw suggested 100 million dollars was barely enough to squeak by on. Okay, I know, people with that kind of money, even people who wish for it, are probably not reading this book. But the principle is the same. What is your "enough"? Do you know? You've thought about it, I suspect, but were either self-aware enough to realize that you probably would not be proud of your answer or in sufficient self-denial to pretend the question was for others and not yourself. What was that word again? Oh yes, "Fool!"

Third, if you agree that life does not consist in the abundance of possessions, what *do* you think life consists in? Family? Country? Church? Not! How about *Love! Valour! Compassion!*? (the title of a play, then movie by Terrence McNally). Closer, even arguably biblical, but still way too abstract. After all, what is being required of us is not just our biological life (Greek *zōē*), but the very principle that makes us alive, our soul (Greek *psuchē*). Our life "consists" in our relationship to God, for us as Christians a relationship defined through Jesus Christ. Everything else, in life and death, flows from and through that or it is less than it might be and will stop with our death.

Finally (okay I lied about three things), perhaps the most important question to ask ourselves: what in the way we lead our lives shows to anyone else what we think life consists in? Not the old, "If you were on trial for being a Christian, would there be enough evidence to convict?" but "Where are you storing up all that makes life, life?"

How did Jesus put it in the Sermon on the Mount? "Do not store up for yourselves treasures on earth, where moth and rust consume and where thieves break in and steal; but store up for yourselves treasures in heaven, where neither moth nor rust consumes and where thieves do not break in and steal. For where your treasure is, there your heart will be also" (Matthew 6:19–21).

The Dishonest Steward: Just When You Think You've Got this Parable Thing Figured Out

> Then Jesus said to the disciples, "There was a rich man who had a manager, and charges were brought to him that this man was squandering his property. So he summoned him and said to him, 'What is this that I hear about you? Give me an accounting of your management, because you cannot be my manager any longer.' Then the manager said to himself, 'What will I do, now that my master is taking the position away from me? I am not strong enough to dig, and I am ashamed to beg. I have decided what to do so that, when I am dismissed as manager, people may welcome me into their homes.' So, summoning his master's debtors one by one, he asked the first, 'How much do you owe my master?' He answered, 'A hundred jugs of olive oil.' He said to him, 'Take your bill, sit down quickly, and make it fifty.' Then he asked another, 'And how much do you owe?' He replied, 'A hundred containers of wheat.' He said to him, 'Take your bill and make it eighty.' And his master commended the dishonest manager because he had acted shrewdly; for the children of this age are more shrewd in dealing with their own generation than are the children of light." (Luke 16:1–8)

This is the weirdest story in the New Testament. Really. If you meet someone who says they know exactly what it means, run away quickly and hold on to your purse or wallet, because most scholars think even Luke was not sure what to make of it. The fun thing about this is that your guess is probably as good as mine, and you are reading this only because I have been guessing about the meaning of the parable of the Dishonest Steward (as it is usually termed) longer than you have. When we are done, we'll pool our hunches and see what we come up with.

Start with the main characters—a steward or manager (Greek *oikonomonos*, like the English "economy") who runs the farming operation of yet another rich person. The amounts involved later in the parable, "a hundred jugs of olive oil" (16:6) and "a hundred containers of wheat" (16:7) are substantial, worth together perhaps as much as one talent, though admittedly this puts us more in mind of the rich farmer we just met than the king in the parable of the Unforgiving Servant (Matt 18:23–35) or the master in the parable of the Talents (Matt 25:14–30). Nevertheless, we are talking about a very wealthy landowner, though not a king or provincial ruler. There are also minor characters, the two who owe debts to the rich man, and the usual onlookers and implied characters, such as whoever it was who told the rich man not to trust his steward. Essentially, though, it is a story about a steward and the rich man he worked for. Questions worth asking, particularly in light of the last parable, are exactly how it was that the man become rich, and what did that mean for his standing in the community, both the community implied in the parable and the community of faith to which Luke addressed his gospel?

We start with a cultural assumption still shared across the ages: prosperity is a blessing, not a curse, and so the presumption must be that wealth is a sign of divine approval, poverty the reverse. There are exceptions, but conventional wisdom from Abraham (Gen 13:2), Solomon (1 Kgs 10:23), and the Psalms ("Happy are those who fear the Lord . . . wealth and riches are in their houses" [112:1, 3]) embraces a version of what we now term, derisively for the most part, the "prosperity gospel." If you love God and keep the commandments, you'll be materially rich.

> We start with a cultural assumption still shared across the ages: prosperity is a blessing, not a curse, and so the presumption must be that wealth is a sign of divine approval, poverty the reverse.

Jesus, however, was not buying it. We have discussed in an earlier chapter the fact that for the most part Jesus took conventional wisdom and turned it on its ear, teaching instead an alternative, indeed subversive wisdom with strong prophetic influences. Jesus was more a "Woe to you who join house to house, who add field to field, until there is room for no one but you" (Isa 5:8) kind of guy than a "God wants you to have a Mercedes Benz like me" type. He did say, "Give, and it will be given to you. A full measure, pressed down, shaken together, running over, will be put in your lap," but somehow those who use this verse to talk about how much God will give their followers forget how the verse ends, "for the measure you give will be the measure you get back" (Luke 6:38).

I chose the Isaiah passage for more than one reason, because it illustrates the particular destructiveness of a kind of greed virulent in an ancient agrarian economy. Which finally brings us to my second point: the only way to get rich was through the land, be it farming, cultivating grapes for wine, or animal husbandry. You could survive by fishing, but that was about it, and the occasional merchant of luxury goods, such as the one we met in Matt 13:45–46, were both few and far between, kept in business by wealthy landowners. The ancient economy was a "zero-sum" economy. Because there were no economies of scale, increases in productivity, or inventions and innovations to create new opportunities, the amount of wealth available was fixed. That meant the way one person got more was if someone else got less. The only way you could expand your land holdings was to somehow acquire the land of someone else. What's wrong with that? Plenty. For one thing, there were no industrial or commercial jobs waiting, so you farmed, fished, or starved. Craft workers, like carpenters, were below farmers in the socioeconomic scheme, in all likelihood eking out a living by woodworking because they had no land to farm. Jubilee laws (Lev 25) were intended to return land holdings to the families who sold them to survive, canceling the debts and reestablishing the patrimony. Despite the command to restructure the economy this way every fifty years, we have no evidence that it ever happened.

This presumption slowly changed, accelerating with each conquest of Palestine, and by Jesus' day had turned entirely, so that by the time of our parable it was presumed that the wealthy got that way at the expense and on the back of others. James put it in typically pithy fashion, "Is it not the rich who oppress you? Is it not they who drag you into court?" (Jas 2:6). Simply beginning a story as Jesus often did, with "there was a certain wealthy person," is to set off alarms. Was this just another crook, an exploiter of the labor of others? How did he get so wealthy, and who did he step on along the way? Was he another absentee landlord, as in Mark 12:1–8, and that's why he needed a steward? Late nineteenth-century American attitudes toward "robber barons" are a rough equivalent of the way first-century Jews felt about rich people.

With this background we return to the story proper. The rich landowner, whether he lived on the property managed by our steward or, as is more likely, in a cosmopolitan Mediterranean city, has been told that the steward is robbing him blind. So he summons the steward and gives him his two-week notice, requiring him to produce the books with a hint of "they had better balance or you are not going to just be unemployed, you're going to jail." The steward is a realist. "What will I do . . . ? I'm not strong enough to dig, and I am ashamed to beg" (Luke 16:3). What he does have going for him is a little time (apparently they did not "perp walk" you in handcuffs out of the office, carting your computer to the FBI or Scotland Yard, in those days).

What the steward decided to do is intriguing, and the source of much confusion. He called in those who owed the boss money (measured in oil and wheat—this is an agrarian economy, remember) and had them, in their own handwriting, help him, uh, "clean up" the books. Genius. Not only does he make the debtors very happy (perhaps happy enough to give him a job or a least a meal or two when his current gig is up), but he also keeps himself out of jail. By reducing the amount owed on the books, he seems to be erasing the amount he had pocketed, while simultaneously reducing the amount owed by the debtors. Everybody is happy except the rich master, who could surely afford to take the loss.

It is the moment of reckoning that confuses. We can understand why the steward and the debtors would be pleased with the changes. But how do we make sense of the master's response: "And his master commended the dishonest manager because he had acted shrewdly" (Luke 16:8)?

A variety of explanations, all of them failures in my opinion, have been offered. The first one is textual. While the NRSV begins 16:8 with a possessive, "*his* master," the Greek uses the definite article, "*the* master" (the possessive is an infrequent, though defensible, choice) and what's more, "master" translates *kyrios*, so it would be just as fair to translate the phrase, "the Lord," or, Jesus. But to do this disconnects the response to the steward's action from the parable itself, and ends the parable at verse 7, making the commendation of the steward a part of the added maxims that begin with the second half of verse 8, "For the children of this age are more shrewd in dealing with their own generation than are the children of light." The series of somewhat related, somewhat not related sayings about the right and wrong use of money in 16:9–13 inspired C. H. Dodd, the author of the definition of the parable we have used throughout this book, to write, "We can almost see here notes for three separate sermons on the parable as text."[3] The problem with this explanation is that it only shifts the difficulty; it does not resolve it. Now, instead of the landowner praising the dishonesty of the steward, it is Jesus doing so. That is supposed to help?

Joachim Jeremias, and many others, fall back on the favorite: "This was a real case brought to Jesus' attention, and he comments on it," an approach that I have recommended we avoid in the case of all parables, and which still leaves us needing to explain why Jesus praises dishonesty. Scholars Dan Via and others go the "picaresque" route, talking about the steward as a "lovable rogue" whose ingenuity impresses his boss, who himself is not always on the right side of the law.[4] And speaking of law, since Torah forbids lending at interest, another explanation is that both the steward and landowner were violating Torah, and in changing the bills the steward was eliminating the prohibited interest. When this came to light in public, the landowner could do nothing but swallow the loss and praise the steward for, in essence, making honest men out of them both.

The **"picaresque"** tradition in literature emphasizes "lovable rogues" who skirt the law for the benefit of a greater good—think Friar Tuck or Sancho Panza.

My guess is that you are no more convinced by any of these explanations than I have been over the years, especially because at one level or another, moral ambiguity, or dishonesty, if not outright criminal behavior is being praised. In church. By Jesus.

When we started looking at the parable of the Dishonest Steward, I claimed that no one, present company included, was sure what we were to take from the story. The sayings added in the verses that follow caution us about the slipperiness and trickiness of money. The last saying reminds that, "You cannot serve God and wealth" (Luke 16:13). But why not? Why can't we use wealth to the glory of God? If I had Warren Buffet's or Sir John Templeton's investment acumen, why couldn't I build a fortune for the church to use for the good of the gospel? I know I hope those investing my retirement funds at the Church Pension Group are keeping up with the returns of those on Wall Street, shrewd as others "in their own generation."

But that is not the point. There is nothing unethical about investment returns that match the Standard and Poors 500 or some other benchmark. This guy was cheating. But cheating whom? Is there perhaps a little bit of Robin Hood going on? I think so, and I don't think it bothered Jesus one bit. He didn't care if Zaccheus' heirs suffered from his decision to restore fourfold what he had immorally acquired, or that his disciples were plucking someone else's grain (let alone that it was on the Sabbath). He didn't even care that a valuable resource that could have been used for the poor was instead used to "anoint him beforehand for burial." Money, frankly, was a matter of indifference, because "life does not consist in the abundance of possessions."

Be careful here. I am not advocating anything. I am simply trying to understand why the apparent defrauding of a rich man was praiseworthy, and I think it must have something to do with the fact that things other than the accumulation of wealth are worthy of praise. Remember also that this is a parable of decision, and lots of decisions were made, at the very least those of the steward, the landowner, Jesus, and Luke. What decision do you make?

The Great Banquet: What's Your Excuse?

One of my favorite ways to avoid making a decision is to come up with an excuse. "It's not that I don't want to, it's that I can't." "If this, that, or the other were different, I would do, be, think . . . whatever . . . in a heartbeat."

> "Someone gave a great dinner and invited many. At the time for the dinner he sent his slave to say to those who had been invited, 'Come; for everything is ready now.' But they all alike began to make excuses. The first said to him, 'I have bought a piece of land, and I must go out and see it; please accept my regrets.' Another said, 'I have bought five yoke of oxen, and I am going to try them out; please accept my regrets.'

Another said, 'I have just been married, and therefore I cannot come.' So the slave returned and reported this to his master. Then the owner of the house became angry and said to his slave, 'Go out at once into the streets and lanes of the town and bring in the poor, the crippled, the blind, and the lame.' And the slave said, 'Sir, what you ordered has been done, and there is still room.' Then the master said to the slave, 'Go out into the roads and lanes, and compel people to come in, so that my house may be filled. For I tell you, none of those who were invited will taste my dinner.'" (Luke 14:16–24)

In a world without refrigeration, microwaves, and convection ovens, not to mention take-out and caterers, dinner parties were different. Who knows how long it takes to roast a whole calf or lamb? It appears that you invited people ahead of time—a week or a day or whatever—and when the food was ready you sent the limousine around to bring them to your house. Or something like that.

In the parable of the Banquet, someone is hosting a "great dinner," quite possibly another rich person, given the expense involved, the presence of servants, and a house that is not easily filled with guests. When everything is ready, a slave is sent to inform the invited guests, maybe as a courtesy, or perhaps as an escort. In any case, it is a narrative necessity creating the conversation by which we learn of the guests' excuses. One needs to inspect property, another wants to test-drive his new oxcart, and a third got married. The excuses are not random, but they are curious. To our ears only the last one seems like a good enough reason not to honor a commitment. Many have pointed out the parallel to Deut 20:5–8, which details legitimate reasons not to join in battle. "Has anyone built a new house but not dedicated it? . . . Has anyone planted a vineyard but not yet enjoyed its fruit? . . . Has anyone become engaged to a woman but not yet married her? He should go back to his house, or he might die in the battle and another marry her." More important than possible sources is what the excuses tell us about at least two of the guests. They too are wealthy; neither land nor oxen, after all, are available for free. Just like you and me, the one giving the party invites his peers, perhaps even some folks from the social class to which he aspires.

And not one of them comes. It is tempting to seek some reason why. Was it social ostracism or repudiation by the community? Was it something he did or something he said? We do not know and it really does not matter. What matters is what he does in response to this rejection. He is angry, of course, but his anger causes him to do something he might never have otherwise done. "Go out at once into the streets and lanes of the town," he orders, "and bring in the poor, the crippled, the blind, and the lame" (Luke 14:21). Does this group sound familiar? It should. There is some basis for maintaining that these outcasts are even cast out of the Temple, considered unclean because they were not whole. Closer to hand, these are among those people whom Isaiah (61:1–2), and Jesus in reading Isaiah and affirming the fulfillment of the Scripture, have embraced. "The Spirit of the Lord is upon me, because he has anointed me to bring good news to the poor. He has sent me to proclaim release to the captives and recovery of sight to the blind, to let the oppressed go free, to proclaim the year of the Lord's favor" (Luke 4:18–19). For the one giving the banquet to command his slave to bring in those usually thought to be cast out is remarkable in every way. Yes, the food would otherwise be wasted, but he could have sent it to the soup kitchen. He didn't have to let them into his house. What's more, when there were still seats vacant he told the slave, "Go out into the roads and lanes and compel people to come in, so that my house may be filled" (Luke 14:23). Who do you suppose that included? Probably the prostitutes, dopers, dealers, and gangbangers. Who else hangs out in the roads and lanes?

There is a cautionary tale here, not unlike that of the parable of the Two Sons with which this chapter began. The guy is mad. "I tell you, none of those who were invited will taste my dinner" (Luke 14:24). Fair enough, and a whole lot better than what the king does in Matthew's version of this story (Matt 22:7). The caution is not to presume upon position. You think your seat is reserved, but if you do not respond when told, "Come, for everything is ready now" you may be in for a surprise. When it comes to the kingdom of God, matters of timing are not up to us. How does the old chestnut go? Everyone wants to go to heaven, but nobody wants to die.

But there is much more than a cautionary tale; there is also an example. Remember my promise not to attend to context? Luke goes out of his way to make that hard to keep. Luke 14:1–24 takes place on the way to, and then at, "the house of a leader of the Pharisees" where Jesus was going "to eat a meal on the sabbath" (14:1). Prior to telling the parable of the Banquet, Jesus had remarked on seating arrangements (14:7–10), cautioned not to invite family and friends when hosting a party because they will return the invitation (14:12–14), and is depicted as sharing the story in response to a fellow dinner guest's proclamation, "Blessed is anyone who will eat bread in the kingdom of God" (14:15). I don't doubt that Jesus agreed, but the parable of the Banquet suggests a more immediate manner of blessing, and might be summarized, "Blessed is the one who provides hospitality to those who cannot return the favor."

The parable of the Banquet is about hospitality. You remember hospitality: inviting friends for a casual supper or impromptu barbecue, welcoming the new neighbors with a dessert or wine and cheese gathering, taking meals to a fellow church member recovering from surgery. Remember? I know, it's been so long ago I might as well mention squeezing the lemons for lemonade and cranking the ice cream churn for a social on the front porch. Now we meet at a restaurant, bring a gift certificate, and send meals-on-wheels. And that's for family and friends. Jesus was talking about strangers. Down-and-out strangers. How well we are ministering to them is the measure of our hospitality.

> You remember hospitality: inviting friends for a casual supper or impromptu barbecue, welcoming the new neighbors with a dessert or wine and cheese gathering, taking meals to a fellow church member recovering from surgery. Remember?

If your church is like my church, we are not measuring up to the standard of the gospel. When unfamiliar faces enter the narthex and walk down the aisle, no one but the designated "greeter" speaks to them, for fear they might be long-time members whose names are forgotten and who are therefore better ignored, lest the collective congregational ignorance be revealed. But far better to over-greet than never meet. Church Hospitality 101 starts with such basic principles, but it does not stop there. It invites, escorts, accompanies, and introduces, reaching out, bringing in, and as it gathers confidence, begins to notice those usually overlooked because they don't look like us.

I'm a realist, so I don't expect you to include the homeless in your next Foyer Group, Supper Club, or family holiday dinner. Hospitality today is different than it was two thousand years ago. However, that does not mean you can be satisfied with dropping a ten instead of a one in the Salvation Army kettle and think you've done your bit. Every congregation has a collective responsibility to respond thoughtfully and prayerfully to the human needs in its wider community, "for you will be repaid at the resurrection of the righteous" (Luke 14:14).

Continuing the Conversation

Two important and related issues—wealth and hospitality—surfaced repeatedly in this chapter, and they merit further attention. Christine Pohl, professor at Asbury Theological Seminary, has written a wonderful book on hospitality, *Making Room: Recovering Hospitality as a Christian Tradition* (Grand Rapids: Eerdmans, 1999). I discuss issues of wealth and possessions in chapter two and five of my commentary on James, *James and Jude,* New Cambridge Bible Commentary (New York: Cambridge University Press, 2004), and recommend Craig Blomberg's *Neither Poverty nor Riches* (Grand Rapids, MI: InterVarsity Press, 2001) and Sondra Wheeler's *Wealth as Peril and Obligation* (Grand Rapids: Eerdmans, 1995).

CHAPTER SIX

In Christ There Is No East nor West: How to Read a Parable for All You're Worth

I have limited goals for this concluding chapter. First, I want to tell you everything you need to know about the Good Samaritan. Then I want to show you how to use what we have learned from reading parables to develop a method for reading all of Scripture. Finally I want to change your life. Ready?

The Good Samaritan: A Long Look at a Short Story

Other than a few categorically cranky types, everyone refers to Luke 10:30–37 as the parable of the Good Samaritan, the cranks calling it an "example story," a category distinction we rejected in the first chapter as unhelpful. Luke gives us a setting that will demand attention later in the chapter (there I go again, planning to consider a parable's context in the gospel when I said I wouldn't—but really, this time it is very important). The story is so well known we could probably skip right over it, but we won't.

> "A man was going down from Jerusalem to Jericho, and fell into the hands of robbers, who stripped him, beat him, and went away, leaving him half dead. Now by chance a priest was going down that road; and when he saw him, he passed

by on the other side. So likewise a Levite, when he came to the place and saw him, passed by on the other side. But a Samaritan while traveling came near him; and when he saw him, he was moved with pity. He went to him and bandaged his wounds, having poured oil and wine on them. Then he put him on his own animal, brought him to an inn, and took care of him. The next day he took out two denarii, gave them to the innkeeper, and said, 'Take care of him; and when I come back, I will repay you whatever more you spend.' Which of these three, do you think, was a neighbor to the man who fell into the hands of the robbers?" He said, "The one who showed him mercy." Jesus said to him, "Go and do likewise." (Luke 10:30–37)

The parable of the Good Samaritan has as many dramatis personae as any story in the gospels. Leaving aside for now Jesus and the lawyer whose questions prompt the telling, we meet an unnamed traveler, presumably Jewish, who is set upon by two or more "robbers" whom we also assume are Jews, for reasons to be explained later. There are two Temple leaders, one a priest and the other a Levite, and so both Jews, and an innkeeper who, given the likely locale, was probably also Jewish. Last but surely not least, the Samaritan, whose status vis-à-vis Judaism is a point of both historical and biblical contention, and that contention is the reason for highlighting that everybody inside and outside the world of the story is Jewish, save one.

Who is our unfortunate victim? We don't know; he is not named, but neither are any of the other characters. We can speculate about why he was going from Jerusalem to Jericho—for business, commercial, legal, or government reasons, to visit family or friends, take a vacation—you name it and it has been suggested by one or another interpreter. And those interpreters will also quickly say that the road from Jerusalem to Jericho was like the road from the Baghdad airport to the Green Zone, famous for its dangerous terrain and even more dangerous brigands. The ancient evidence for this claim outside the parable itself is nonexistent, and unless one is determined to again claim that Jesus was commenting on an actual occurrence (Jeremias), it does not matter. The danger depicted in the narrative world of our story is all the danger we need.

> The road from Jerusalem to Jericho was like the road from the Baghdad airport to the Green Zone, famous for its dangerous terrain and even more dangerous brigands.

Down the road our traveler comes (it is, literally, a descent to Jericho, hard by the Dead Sea, from just about anywhere), only to be set upon by "robbers." These are curious robbers, however, for while they "stripped him, beat him, and went away, leaving him half dead" (Luke 10:30), Jesus did not say that they robbed him. More importantly, the Greek term to describe the ne'er-do-wells, *lēistais*, is not completely translated by the NRSV "robbers," because the term has a political edge to it. It is the term used in the Greek translation of Jeremiah quoted by Jesus in condemning the business activity in the Temple, "It is written, 'My house shall be called a house of prayer'; but you have made it a den of robbers" (Luke 19:46) and, while Luke uses the term "criminals" to describe the two crucified beside Jesus (the Greek, *kakourgoi*, means literally "evildoers"), Matthew and Mark use *lēistoi*. Why does this matter? Because the Romans did not crucify robbers. Crucifixion was limited to those accused of one or another form of insurrection or rebellion against Roman authority. I am not claiming that the Romans did not apply capital punishment much more widely than is customary nowadays, but that there were much simpler ways to execute thieves. Crucifixion, an especially brutal, slow, and agonizing form of execution, requiring the efforts of many soldiers for an extended period (recall the gospel accounts), was used to send a message to the wider population that rebellion would be crushed. It has been described as an act of state terrorism to terrify the population into obedience, an important tool of the "Pax Romana."

All of this is to say that the robbers who did not rob the man on the road to Jericho were not thieves but insurrectionaries, or terrorists. What they did was not about financial gain but about sending a message of their own, and we know from the way the story unfolds that at least two people got the message. Those two, the priest and the Levite, deserve a good bit of attention themselves.

We know from the description of the duties of the father of John the Baptist, Zechariah, in Luke 1:5–23 as well as from extra-biblical sources, that service in the Temple was not limited to a permanent cohort of functionaries, but that members of the various priestly families rotated in and out of service throughout the year. We do not know in which direction the two were traveling, from or toward Jerusalem, which may matter for one explanation of their behavior.

Luke uses a wonderful term, *antiparerxomai*, which the NRSV translates "passed by on the other side" (Luke 10:31, 32), but we could say, "crossed the street to avoid him" to keep the strong "anti" language found in our text. But why? Why did they go out of their way to avoid the injured man?

Explanations abound, and you should feel free to pick your favorite. We could start with human nature. You don't have to be especially squeamish to recoil at the sight of a bloodied body, nor a coward to see the body as a sign of danger to be avoided. Those looking for a deeper reason point to the fact that contact with a corpse is ritually defiling (Leviticus 22:4 and elsewhere) and if the priest were on the way to serve in the Temple, touching what looked like a dead body would make him unable to perform his priestly functions until he himself had been ritually cleansed. This, frankly, strikes me as a stretch in many ways. It does not explain the reaction of the Levite, whose duties were different and would not have been effected, and it presumes that priests did not always ritually prepare prior to their service. More importantly, it is an unnecessary layer of explanation, because it does not matter why they passed the traveler by, just that they did.

One explanation, however, that must be rejected is the one that says that "the priest and the Levite did not stop and help the injured man because they were just a couple of pious hypocrites more worried about saving their own skins than their moral obligation to help anyone in need." Trading on the idea that Jesus' audience expected nothing better from religious leaders is unfounded. What Jesus was after is as great a contrast as he can make between the audience's expectation and how his story will unfold. The surprise finish depends on depicting characters who were admired and respected, here the priest and the Levite, acting selfishly or indifferently. If the audience reacted, "Well, what can you expect from the likes of those jerks who work at the Temple?" the story collapses before it is finished.

Exit, then, the respected if not necessarily popular, members of the religious establishment. Who next? The audience knows the rule of three as well as the storyteller, so someone else will surely come along. Who might it be? A prophet? A proselyte? Maybe a Pharisee, one who upholds the Law more rigorously than even the priest and the Levites. I'll bet that's who it is, reminding us that this reforming movement within Judaism had its heroes despite our unjustified habit of viewing all Pharisees as hypocrites.

But it is not a Pharisee, or anyone else the audience admired. It is a "Samaritan." We do not, frankly, know a lot about the Samaritans. Tradition, if not history, identifies them as the people not deemed important enough to be led into captivity in the Assyrian exile, and so they remained on Mount Gerizim, or Samaria. John specifically tells us in an aside, "Jews do not share things in common with the Samaritans" (John 4:9), and part of the impact of Jesus' conversation with the woman at the well in John 4 is the fact that she is a Samaritan. We know that they held only the "five books of Moses," the Torah, as canonical or binding, and that they did not recognize Jerusalem as the place of worship (John 4:20), because it was not given by Moses. Jesus instructed the disciples when they were going on a kind of trial run as missionaries to "enter no town of the Samaritans" (Matt 10:5), and an unnamed Samaritan village "did not receive him, because his face was set for Jerusalem" (Luke 9:53), but it is not clear what that means beyond some level of opposition.

Taking together what we do know, we can say that Jesus was going for maximum rhetorical impact. The audience was expecting a Pharisee, maybe a scribe, but certainly a lay person in contrast with the priest and Levite. They got the opposite of what they were expecting. Then, just as the first two went out of their way to avoid the injured man, the Samaritan goes out of his way to help him. He provides first aid ("bandaged his wounds, having poured oil and wine on them" [Luke 10:34]), transportation, the cost of professional care (in an inn where he himself might well not have been able to stay), and the promise to repay the innkeeper for whatever additional expenses are incurred (10:35).

The impact of the story depends in part on the sharpness of the contrast between audience expectation and the actual narrative climax. Jesus' audience was expecting a trio that went something like "priest, Levite, Pharisee." A scratchy old recording of Clarence Jordan's "Cotton-Patch Version" featured an evangelist and song leader driving by an injured white man on a rural Southern road, and a black man stopping to help. Any interreligious or racial/ethnic difference will do, I suppose, but after a while they become their own cliché. There is another contrast worth thinking about.

THE VIEW FROM THE DITCH

As we will see when we look at the context placed around the story, there is an understandable tendency to decide that when Jesus said, "Go and do likewise," he included us in the exhortation. No matter our opinion about the legal profession, we find ourselves identifying with the lawyer, and see the example of the Samaritan being the example we are to follow. No, we don't stop every time we see an injured person in the road, but we read the story from the perspective of one having the power to do so if we choose. The force of the story therefore is taken as an encouragement to choose to help more often. That is a good Christian attitude. We are the ones who can make a difference—change the world, even—if only we would decide to do so.

But what if we are not the Samaritan? What if instead we look at the story from the perspective of the man traveling from Jerusalem to Jericho, and find ourselves lying in a ditch, naked, beaten, bloodied, and afraid? How does the world look from the ditch? What if we are the one passed by? After the second time, do we slide into despair, unable to help ourselves and convinced that no one will stop to help us? Put differently, if the question is "Who is my neighbor?" and the answer is, "The neighbor is one who will stop and help you," what limits would you choose to put on the concept "neighbor"? You certainly would not want to limit it to the people who happen to live in dwellings adjacent to your own, or across the street. One reading of much of the instructions about community in the New Testament is that be it Jesus, Paul, the Evangelists, or terms like brother, sister, neighbor, beloved, and so on, all refer to Christians, distinguishing those with faith in Christ from those outside the Church. All the references to loving one another are thereby understood as limited to the community of the faithful. That is a defensible reading of many passages, but not this one. This one, especially viewed from the ditch, repudiates that reading. If you are in need and a neighbor is one who responds to your need, would you in any way want to limit that response by race, gender, ethnicity, creed, or any other division? On the back of your driver's license next to the organ donor box, do you want a place to check the race,

How does the world look from the ditch? What if we are the one passed by?

gender, and religion of the doctor you will allow to treat you? Viewed from the ditch, "neighbor" is anybody who will help.

The Samaritan helped. But first he had to do two things, or at least do one and be open to the other. As a seminary classmate pointed out a generation ago, unlike the priest and Levite, the Samaritan stopped. He stopped. Wherever he was going, whatever he was doing, however big a hurry he was in, he stopped. And then, because he was willing to stop, he could see the situation for what it was, and realized that the fellow in the ditch was injured, not dead, and when he took in the situation, "he was moved with pity" (Luke 10:33). By now you may recall what a pitiful translation that is for the Greek *esplangnisthē*, "have compassion." As we said of the Prodigal's father, he was "moved to the depth of his being." Because he was willing to stop, he could see what was really going on. And because of the sort of person he was, he had compassion. Without both stopping and having compassion, *we* would still be lying in the ditch.

IMAGINE THAT: A LAWYER WANTING TO JUSTIFY HIMSELF

"The first thing we do," said the character in Shakespeare's *Henry VI*, is "kill all the lawyers" (part 2, act 4, scene 2). Ouch. What did they ever do to poor old William? Maybe nothing. Maybe Shakespeare was familiar with the context of the parable of the Good Samaritan, and shared the antipathy widely expressed about the lawyer in Luke 10:25–37. I'll be the first to admit, he gets off to a bad start. "Just then a lawyer stood up to test Jesus. 'Teacher,' he said, 'what must I do to inherit eternal life?'" (Luke 10:25). This is the same verb—"test"—used to describe Jesus' temptation in the wilderness and quoted by Jesus, "Do not put the Lord your God to the test" (Luke 4:2, 12). But it happens. The scribes, lawyers, and Pharisees are trying to figure out who Jesus is and what to do with him. So the lawyer asked, and asked a question others, like the man with many possessions (Mark 10:17), ask Jesus, too. But when you stop and think about it, other than Luke's characterization, what is wrong with the question? If you had one question to ask Jesus, wouldn't that be the one? But it is not the "testing," or the question itself, that we get on him about, it is the line (again from Luke) that follows the dialogue about the Law. "But wanting to justify himself, he asked Jesus, 'And who is my neighbor?'"(Luke 10:29). Ugh, that is awful. Wanting to *justify* himself? Disgusting!

Or is it? The verb, *dikaioō* in the infinitive, is *the* term to describe and define being made right with God. Luke uses it to describe the tax collector we met in chapter four, the one who could barely stammer out a prayer asking for mercy yet went home "justified" (Luke 18:14). And it is the term Paul uses more than twenty times to describe what God has done for the world in giving his only begotten Son. To be justified is synonymous with "inheriting eternal life." So maybe we should give the lawyer a break. Looked at differently, all he is doing is asking the question we would ask Jesus if we had the chance, and then, realizing what was at stake, wanting to make sure he understood. Is that so bad? Of course, having done so, he gets to deal with the close of the encounter—go and do likewise.

MARTHA, MARTHA, MARTHA

Most New Testament scholars agree that the context for reading the parable of the Good Samaritan is not only the dialogue with the lawyer, but the short story of Mary and Martha that follows. The rationale doesn't come from evidence within the text, for there is no overwhelming transition or change in direction taking place. Chapters ten and eleven are part of the journey to Jerusalem. But there is an important sense in which the story of Mary and Martha provides balance to our understanding of what it means to "go and do likewise."

> Now as they went on their way, he entered a certain village, where a woman named Martha welcomed him into her home. She had a sister named Mary, who sat at the Lord's feet and listened to what he was saying. But Martha was distracted by her many tasks; so she came to him and asked, "Lord, do you not care that my sister has left me to do all the work by myself? Tell her then to help me." But the Lord answered her, "Martha, Martha, you are worried and distracted by many things; there is need of only one thing. Mary has chosen the better part, which will not be taken away from her." (Luke 10:38–42)

Jesus comes to dinner. The one and only Jesus. Luke tells us nothing about Lazarus, but we assume this is the same family as in John 11, and whether this incident takes place before or after Lazarus' death and raising is unknown and unimportant. What matters is that Jesus is here, and of course, he has brought a crowd with him.

Remember the discussion of hospitality in the last chapter? Well, this scene is not for anyone who flunked Hospitality 101. This is the advanced course. The phrase "a woman named Martha welcomed him into her home" is loaded. Even if we limit ourselves to contemporary notions of what that means, you know the drill: cleaning, cooking (or coordinating the caterers), arranging flowers and furniture, maybe cadging extra chairs and a table or two, and, depending on your generation, polishing the silver or buying the fancy paper napkins to match the Chinette. Then you have to figure out the seating arrangements, select the wine, and pray that it doesn't rain or everyone will be forced inside. Of *course* Martha was distracted! Every time we throw a dinner party at our house my wife and I are reminded why we do not do it more often.

But that is the contemporary way. When you welcomed someone into your home in ancient Mediterranean culture, you added a member to your family, which was not a problem with Jesus—it was the twelve other guys who moved in with him, not to mention assorted other followers. I'll say she was distracted.

Here's the real kicker. Martha was distracted by her "ministry." The term, *diakonia* (modified by *polla*, "much"), is the technical term for servant ministry in the New Testament, and our term "deacon" is directly derived from it. Martha was ministering to Jesus and it was a source of distraction. Other women are described as ministering to Jesus (Matt 27:55, gathered at the foot of the cross), and in almost every other reference to *diakonia*, from the ministry of Stephen and the six (Acts 6), throughout Paul's letters, even in the Book of Revelation (2:19), servant ministry is a very good thing.

Yet Mary, sitting at Jesus' feet, has apparently made the better choice of what to do with her life, "which will not be taken away from her" (Luke 10:42). Who saw that coming?

On a practical level we have to admire Jesus' good sense, shown here and later in Luke (12:13–14), not to get in the middle of family disputes. Let the siblings work it out. But after all that business about "go and do likewise," it seems a little harsh to just leave Martha alone to do the heavy lifting. Would it kill Mary to lend a hand for a few minutes? Or is that not the point?

> We have to admire Jesus' good sense, shown here and later in Luke, not to get in the middle of family disputes. Let the siblings work it out.

Go back to how the story begins: Jesus is here—*here*, in Martha's house. How often do you think that is going to happen? If Jesus came to your house, what would you do? Sit down and listen to what he had to say or spend the day in the kitchen preparing a gourmet meal? Who is trying to impress whom with their *diakonia*? Moreover, Mary is depicted as adopting the posture of a disciple (*mathētēs*), sitting at the feet of her master. When it comes to a choice between discipleship and ministry, we need to be careful what we choose.

The late Jesuit teacher, writer, and retreat leader, Anthony deMello, told of a call to a Lama for help, and the Lama sends five monks in response. One by one the monks drop off, one to marry, one to be a king, another to help a monastery, all choosing to do very good things, but not the thing they were sent to do. Finally the fifth arrives to provide the help requested. DeMello points out that nothing distracts us from our calling like our religion.[1]

The story also serves as a useful corrective to the call to action implicit in most readings of the Good Samaritan. Jesus, after all, does not say "Go and be," but "Go and *do*." But the first thing the Samaritan did was nothing. He stopped. So did Mary, while Martha rushed around the house, presumably not hearing a thing Jesus had to say. When our service gets in the way of our hearing what Jesus has to say, it is time for us to stop as well. How does the Buddhist saying go? Don't just do something, sit there.

From Parable to Scripture

Do you know you have a hermeneutic? You do. Hermeneutics is the study of the interpretive principles that undergird the way we read anything, be it Scripture, the phone book, a novel, or a vanity license plate. Most of the time we read quite well without paying any attention to the principles we are using. When it comes to the phone book, we know that last names come first, the short series of numbers followed by a simple word or two, "223 Robin Rd.," is an address, and the longer series of numbers with a dash in between the third and fourth is the telephone number. We even know that an initial instead of a first name, "B." instead of "Bill," likely means that "B." is Barbara or Bonnie. We use our imaginations when reading a novel, allowing things

> Hermeneutics is the study of the interpretive principles that undergird the way we read anything, be it Scripture, the phone book, a novel, or a vanity license plate.

to happen that would violate our sense of history or science (Harry Potter!), but use our imaginations differently when "reading" a vanity license plate. My favorite was on a vintage Porsche—RUNVS. (I was.)

We use this same take-it-for-granted approach to Scripture. We know that the Psalms are poetry, Deuteronomy has lots of laws, and the books with weird names are probably books of prophecy. Generally speaking we do not scrutinize the Bible for recipes, scientific theory, or American history, and if we meet someone who does, whether we know it or not, what we question is their hermeneutic. People who want to know how many inches in a cubit so they can rebuild the Ark are probably missing the point. The story of Noah is not written to provide guidance for a naval shipyard but as a reiteration of the divine covenant with creation.

To get the point of a passage, you often need to be self-conscious about your hermeneutic—your principles of interpretation. These principles first help you read biblical literature differently depending on genre. Just as Sci-Fi and Harlequin romances require different approaches, we read the maxims in Proverbs differently than the poetry in Psalms, and both of them differently than the narrative history of Israel and Judah in the books of Samuel and Kings. And to the point at hand, we read parables differently than we read other genres found in Scripture. However, starting with the Mary and Martha story as example, I suggest we may benefit greatly by applying what we have learned from reading parables to how we read almost all of Scripture.

I have called it the "story of Mary and Martha" because despite its likeness to other narrative descriptions of events in this gospel, Luke 10:38–42 "works" as story—indeed as a short story not unlike other short stories in the Bible, such as Jonah and Ruth (in case you missed it, I just made a huge hermeneutical leap—more later). And like other short stories, in and out of Scripture, I read it much as I read a parable. I am not worried about where the people lived, in a way I am not even worried *if* they lived. That is, I am not going to launch an archeological dig in Bethany for Mary's and Martha's house in the hope of finding all the dirty dishes Mary wouldn't wash and thereby "prove" that the story is "true." Its truth is at a different level. Just as the important turn in the Good Samaritan was the different reactions to the injured man by the priest/Levite and Samaritan, the juxtaposition of the two sisters' response to having Jesus under their roof, *and* the juxtaposition of Jesus' responses to the lawyer and to Martha, is the key to understanding the meaning of the narrative. Some parable interpreters argue that Jesus heard about an injured man helped by a Samaritan and used it as an example of neighborliness for the lawyer, an approach that suggests if someone could prove that it was actually the road to Bethlehem and not Jericho, the story would not be true. That level of historicity is foreign to the gospels, and I think for the most part foreign to Scripture.

This reveals one of my foundational principles for interpreting Scripture: the Bible is the Word of God because it speaks God's truth to all peoples for all time, not because it can be demonstrated to be historically accurate to a given time and place. For all I know, Luke could have gotten Mary and Martha's names backwards, and it was *Mary* who was distracted by her servant ministry. That would not make Luke 10:38–42 less true as far as I am concerned, nor less inspired by the Holy Spirit. To others what I just wrote is evidence of my heretical lack of commitment to the inerrancy and infallibility of the Bible.

> The Bible is Word of God because it speaks God's truth to all peoples for all time, not because it can be demonstrated to be historically accurate to a given time and place.

The parables of Jesus teach us that richness of meaning and importance for faithful Christian living is not limited to our appropriation of historical facts and theological doctrines. The parables, by their very openness to more than one interpretation (the difference between looking at the Good Samaritan from the perspective of the lawyer or from the guy lying in the ditch), teach us that Jesus *liked* polyvalency (multiple-meanings); in fact, Jesus thrived on it, according to all four Evangelists. So how in heaven did the faithfulness of the followers of Jesus become defined by an insistence on a single, historicized, read-it-like-I-do-or-you're-going-to-heck approach to Scripture?

A fair question to ask is what a "parabolic hermeneutic" looks like when applied to biblical material manifestly non-parabolic. To stay fairly close to home, consider the Sermon on the Mount, Matt 5–7, which concludes with the short parable of the Two Foundations and is otherwise also entirely filled with metaphor, simile, analogy, hyperbole, comparison, and other forms also found in parable. If we focus in on Matt 5:17–48, we find a series of "antitheses" ("you have heard it said, but I say to you") bounded by extraordinary sayings about

Jesus fulfilling the Law and the Prophets and his followers being called to "be perfect as your heavenly Father is perfect." The sayings quote Torah on murder, adultery, divorce, swearing an oath, vengeance, and love for neighbor and elaborate by comparing anger to murder, lust to adultery and divorce, and insisting on simple speech, forbearance, and love of the enemy. When we consider the implications of what Jesus is calling for, we cannot help but think, "That's impossible, nobody's perfect." But Jesus said, "You must be perfect."

What do we do with a command to be what we cannot be? It is an important question because such commands are everywhere, not only in the Sermon on the Mount but throughout the parables and the rest of Scripture. Go back to a verse I described in the last chapter as my favorite memory verse for those who insist that all Scripture must be read literally, Luke 14:33: "None of you can become my disciple unless you give up all your possessions." Jesus could not possibly mean us to take this literally, could he? We'd all be broke. But it is a very clear statement, just as clear as prohibitions against divorce, adultery, and homosexual activity in the Old Testament. The *hermeneutical* issue is to determine the basis upon which you decide to read one command literally and binding across all time, and another as not. I said it was important.

The appeal to parable as a model for reading is to free us from a rote literalism that privileges one reading to the exclusion of all others, and makes our approach to Scripture a perpetual choice between right and wrong. That is always a false choice, because it is always more complicated than right and wrong readings. It was more complicated than that two millennia ago reading a Greek papyrus or Hebrew scroll. Now, scores of copyings, translations, a Reformation or two, and a century of archeological discoveries later, it is more complicated than ever.

Parables require a suppleness, a lightness of reading that we do well to apply to much of the rest of Scripture. Parable invites us to look at longer narrative threads, to see how the large stories of Scripture speak in ways that our tendency to focus on individual readings does not. For instance, when we read passages from Genesis, we may enjoy this or that episode from the lives of Abraham, Isaac, Jacob, and Joseph, but we are not especially aware of the broader narrative telling us how the "chosen people" came to dwell in Egypt, nor of the parallel narratives of Sarah and Hagar, Rebekah, Leah and Rachel, and Dinah. Rarely do we attend to the even broader narrative of election and establishment, apostasy and exile, repentance and restoration, that moves throughout Scripture from "Generations to Revolutions," as the late Baptist pastor Clarence Cranford would say.

The parabolic hermeneutic also "works" in two places you might not imagine—the laws of Deuteronomy and Leviticus and the theology of Paul. Most conversations, and all arguments, about the place of the moral and ritual codes in Torah center on the question of what is still relevant for Christian conduct and what is so inextricably tied to ancient Judaism as to be helpful today only for understanding Israelite religion. These readings inevitably deal with individual laws, so we keep the Sabbath (actually we mostly do not) but we do not keep the dietary laws, yet we do not understand the story that the laws themselves are telling. Leviticus 13 and 14 devote 116 verses— more verses than the entire Letter of James—to the detection, treatment, and ritual cleansing of skin diseases. What is that all about? And if we do not ask the larger narrative question of the story the laws tell, how will we know? The narrative of Paul's theology is also lost in discussion of, say, his approach to the role of women in the life of the community. We forget to unpack his rhetoric when arguing about whether we agree with what he said, but if we don't understand how he said what he said, and how that fits into the larger movement of his theology—from sin to salvation by the grace of God in Jesus Christ—we lose the meaning in the argument.

Along the way I hope I have suggested at least a couple of readings of familiar parables that never occurred to you before. Does that mean that you were WRONG to only view the Good Samaritan from the privileged perspective of one who gets to choose for whom and when you will use your capacity to help persons in need? No, no more than you were WRONG to think of yourself as fertile or infertile soil in the allegory of the Seed and the Soils, or as either the younger or older brother (but certainly not the father) in the parable of the Prodigal.

Readings and interpretations vary widely. But it is not a simple choice between right and wrong. Rather it has to do with which interpretation is more persuasive. I do not need to prove an interpretation of this, that, or the other to be wrong. I need to persuade you that my approach more fully accounts for how folks lived, prayed, thought, and taught then, and how we are called to do so now.

Reading a Parable for All You Are Worth

Reading parables is fun. Not going to Disney World kind of fun, but reading fun. When a parable "works"—and they don't always work for everyone—it does indeed "arrest the hearer by its vividness or strangeness" and "tease" the mind into active thought by "leaving the mind in sufficient doubt about its precise application." Parables are fun because the reader has to do some work, there is a riddle that needs to be solved, a paradox explained, a behavior understood.

Helping you understand the mechanics and dynamics of twenty-five or so parables of Jesus was the first goal of the book. Suggesting that reading the rest of Scripture with the same level of engagement and openness to more than one way of reading a passage was a second goal. But to what end? Is it enough to understand what a truly weird story the parable of the Dishonest Steward is, or to learn that, despite the apparent evidence of the parable of the Rich Fool, Jesus does not hate rich people? I suppose so, if knowledge is an end in itself. I am not convinced that knowing the Bible is the goal. The water, as Teresa of Avila wrote, is for the flowers.[2] If nothing is different in our lives of faith because we understand the parables, what is the point of our newfound understanding? Nothing. Finally, I think, we must stop reading the parables and let the parables read us.

Over the years I have tried to resist the temptation to do all the good things I am invited to do in ministry and be both more disciplined and focused in what I do and what I ask people in my parish to do. I have reflected in meetings, retreats, and in writing on the topic of what matters in ministry, and have decided that there are only five things that matter—prayer, Scripture, worship, guidance, and witness.[3] If I cannot discern how what I am asked to do, or am doing in ministry, relates to one of the five things that matters, then there is an excellent chance that I probably should not be doing it, nor asking others in the parish to do so. It may be very worthwhile, healthy, and wholesome, or just a nice thing to do, but it is not prayer, Scripture, worship, guidance, or witness, so it is not ministry. Since my vocation is ministry, and not social work, psychological therapy, political lobbying, or lots of other good and important things, I find I say "no" a lot. People hate that in clergy.

It should not surprise you to learn that my reading of the parables greatly informed my decisions about what matters in ministry. By way of explaining what I mean by "letting the parables read us," I'll conclude by looking at how the parables suggest the shape of ministry, indeed of Christian life, in each of the five things that matter.

PRAYER

We start with prayer because that is where ministry starts. Two parables considered in chapter four, the Persistent Widow (Luke 18:1–8) and the Pharisee and Tax Collector (Luke 18:9–14), teach us much of what we need to know about prayer, complete with Luke's preface telling us what we are to take from the parables. From the first, we "need to pray always and to not lose heart" and from the second that we should not "trust in ourselves and regard others with contempt." Pray always. Paul says the same thing, "Pray without ceasing" (1 Thess 5:17). How in heaven are we to do that? And not lose heart? Has Luke been paying attention? People are dying, terrorists threatening, oil prices climbing, schools faltering, and my back hurts. How am I supposed to not lose heart? I suppose by praying without ceasing so I don't have the time to lose heart. The problem here is that we think of praying as saying stuff to God, and we imagine that God thinks of praying as saying stuff to us. We need to look at it from God's perspective: shut up, and listen. Can you listen without ceasing, attending to God's presence and way in the world? Can you try? Good. Then when you get good at it, don't trust it, and don't look down on those who don't pray continually as well as you. But keep listening. Because God knows what you need before you ask (Matthew 6:8), but you don't know what God is saying unless you listen.

SCRIPTURE

Where did I learn that? From Scripture, of course, which is the second thing that matters in ministry. Scripture, interpreted in communion with God and in community with others, is the ever-available schoolhouse of faith. But it is not a mine to be searched for nuggets to use in our arguments, hoping to prove our point by having a bigger stack of verses on our side than the stack of those with whom we disagree. We live in, and with, Scripture. It is the Pearl of Great Price (Matt 13:45–46) for which we sell everything, not to put it on the mantle but to put it to use in everything we say and do. When we combine prayer and Scripture (*lectio divina*—a patient, passionate, and contemplative approach to Scripture, reading with "all your heart, and with all your soul, and with all your might" [Deut 6:5]), then we really have something, listening as God speaks to us through the Word.

That is tough to beat, but there are those who think otherwise. What do we do with them? We need to recall the parable of the Wheat and Weeds (Matt 13:24–30) and remind ourselves that it takes all kinds to make up a Kingdom, including people whose interpretation of Scripture differs from ours. It wouldn't be much of a Kingdom if everyone agreed all the time, anyway.

WORSHIP

The third thing that matters in ministry—the central thing—is worship. If the chief end of humanity is to "glorify God and enjoy God forever," worship is the chief way we do it. We do it in all kinds of ways—formally, liturgically, and in silent awe at a summer sunset. Mostly we do not do it enough, taking worship for granted, knowing that at eight o'clock and ten o'clock on Sunday it is waiting for us, like the Banquet was waiting for the invited guests (Luke 14:16–24) who were too busy to come, and so others were invited. But for those others, worship can be like the mustard seed, not all that much to start with but will you get a load of the end results. A few songs, a prayer, some Scripture read and explored, a scrap of bread and a sip of wine, which becomes in them "a spring of water gushing up into eternal life" (John 4:14).

GUIDANCE

The fourth thing that matters is guidance, in all sorts of ways, from catechism and formation to pastoral care, spiritual direction, and homiletical admonition. Funny thing about guidance, however. It is not instruction or teaching so much as accompaniment and mentoring. People need someone to walk with them on the journey of faith, not one more person to tell them what to think, do, or believe. Ministry is about guidance, and not on silly little nothing issues, but on the big ones of life and death and what to do in the meantime. Like what to do with our wealth and possessions, so that we do not find ourselves like the Rich Fool (Luke 12:16–20), on the night of our death wishing we had spent more time at the office. Or like the Rich Man who overlooked not only Lazarus, but Moses and the prophets, and found himself in a world of torment and regret (Luke 16:19–31).

WITNESS

Finally comes witness, last but not least but nevertheless last, because without prayer, Scripture, worship, and guidance, our witness often loses its way. We witness in lots of ways, looking for lost sheep, coins, and children (Luke 15), casting the seed of God's love with abandon (Mark 4:3–9), and doing unto the least of these (Matt 25:31–46). The parables teach us to emphasize hospitality in our ministry (Luke 14:12–24), but to take care that we do not limit our hospitality to those who can and will reciprocate.

Prayer. Scripture. Worship. Guidance. Witness. Everything I needed to know about what matters in ministry I learned from the parables of Jesus.

Prayer. Scripture. Worship. Guidance. Witness.

Everything I needed to know about what matters in ministry I learned from the parables of Jesus.

Continuing the Conversation

A good place to continue the conversation on hermeneutics without actually having to read about hermeneutics is Marcus Borg's *Reading the Bible Again for the First Time* (San Francisco: Harper SanFrancisco, 2002). As he does in all his books, including one for this series, Marcus writes in a splendidly accessible manner that the rest of us envy and try to emulate, usually without success. Now that we are at the end of *this* conversation, I also want to mention an important source book for understanding not only the world of the parables, but the ancient Mediterranean world in general, Bruce Malina's *The New Testament World*, now in its third edition (Louisville: Westminster John Knox Press, 2001).

ACKNOWLEDGMENTS

There is nothing like being present at the creation. In my role as Associate Director of the Louisville Institute (a grant-making and convening program of the Religion Division of the Lilly Endowment, Inc.), I met with Debra Farrington and Fred Schmidt, and then with a group of authors, rectors, and parish educators to envision how this series might best serve the needs of the Church. To Debra and Fred, and to the Louisville Institute and its Executive Director, Jim Lewis, we all owe a word of gratitude.

Every writer owes thanks to many people. My debt to John R. Donahue, S.J., who in a classroom at Vanderbilt Divinity School completely overwhelmed me with the parables of Jesus, is apparent on every page. After Vanderbilt many teachers and colleagues shaped my understanding. In Chicago I must mention *mein Doktorvater* (dissertation adviser) Arthur J. Droge, Hans Dieter Betz, Michael Murrin, and over lunches, Dom Crossan. If one is known by the company they keep, I have been blessed as a writer to keep company with Marcus Borg, Barbara Taylor, Nora Gallagher, Tom Long, Lauren Winner, and Dr. Fred Craddock. Parishes in Pittsburgh; Chicago; Mansfield, Ohio; Rochester, New York; and Louisville, Kentucky, have listened, questioned, and shaped me and this book. Thank you all.

Nancy Fitzgerald, Ryan Masteller, and the Rev. Helen McPeak have enriched this series and this volume by their careful reading, critical questions, and relentless deadlines. Blessings!

Finally—and why in heaven is this always last?—to my beloved girls, Christine and Emily, for listening to me pontificate about the parables at the supper table, blessing my escapes to get the writing done, and following me to the ends of the earth, ¡Gracias!

STUDY QUESTIONS

the Reverend Helen McPeak

William Brosend brings rich scholarship and playful authenticity to this lively study of Jesus' parables. With vivid imagery and crisp thought, he brings his own experience of family and faith community into conversation with generations of teaching, and demands of his reader thoughtful engagement and an openness to the in-breaking of the Spirit of God.

Introduction

Before you begin Brosend's text, take some time to reflect on experiences with stories in your life.
- Who told/tells you stories? When? Where?
- How are stories a part of your life now?

Pray together for God's guidance and support in this study you are beginning.
- What do you hope to learn?
- Why do you engage it now?
- How will you open yourself to receive what God is giving?

Brosend suggests, "You should be very, very glad if your priest believes in [inductive preaching]" because you are likely to experience creativity and exploration and a wonderful sense of discovery (p. xiii).
- What sermons stay in your memory days, weeks, even years after you hear them?
- What worked about them?
- What was last Sunday's sermon about?

Brosend asserts that sermons and parables are *oral*—meant to be heard, not read (p. xiii).

- In what parts of your life are stories spoken?
- Who tells tales and reads aloud in your life?
- To whom do you offer spoken stories?

Read a parable aloud now. Read to a child as soon as possible.

Brosend writes, "There is something about the way we must approach the parables—reverently but not rigorously, seriously but not literally, expecting to discover something we did not know and to be delighted in both the process and product—that can be usefully applied to the Psalter, prophets, epistles, even Torah and history" (p. xiv).

- How were you taught to approach Scripture?
- What guidance was offered as you engaged holy writings? By whom?
- How is that serving you today?

Chapter One
I Love to Tell the Story: Jesus the Storyteller

Brosend writes, "There is a distinction between story and history, but in the Bible it is neither always clear nor finally absolute. Before and after we ask, 'Did it happen?' we must ask, 'What does it mean?' because as people of faith we are seekers after the truth, and not just the facts" (p. 2).

- What definition of "story" does he offer in the following paragraphs? (See p. 2.)
- What two reasons does Brosend explore in the following pages for Jesus' using parables? (See p. 2–3.)
- How great is your own need for "individual, if not remedial, tutoring"?

Did you run screaming from the room when Brosend named it: *polyvalency*?

- What definition does he offer for this concept? (See p. 4.)
- What other definitions can you find? (Not even www.wiki pedia.com is of much help here. Go to the library. Call up

a seminary professor or other biblical scholar.) How do these inform your understanding of parables?

■ How is it for you to embrace this possibility?

Explore the main movements Brosend outlines in the history of parable interpretation (pp. 5–9).

■ What strengths and weaknesses can you name in each?
■ With which movements do you resonate?

In his "introduction to the introduction," Brosend unpacks Vernon Robbins's five textures found in any and every biblical text (pp. 8–11).

■ What are these textures?
■ What is the focus of each, the boundary of exploration?
■ Which have you experienced as particularly helpful? With which do you struggle?

Brosend claims C. H. Dodd's definition of parables for use in this study.

■ Revisit it on page 11.
■ How would you express this definition if you were making an illustrated medieval text of these words? What pictographs would express it? How would you draw it in Pictionary?

Try it now, on newsprint with lots of color, texture, and shape. Be sure to include all five qualities of parables that Dodd elucidates. (See pp. 11–16.)

Brosend offers some warnings about using this definition. Look at his explorations of each quality of a parable.

■ What does Brosend say about assuming too much similarity between our lives and common life of first-century Palestine? (See pp. 12–13.)
■ What does he say about cultural and historical differences? (See pp. 12–13.)
■ What is said about ignoring multiple versions of a story? (See p. 14.)
■ What does Brosend say about locking ourselves into the same interpretation every time we encounter a parable? (See p. 15.)

What is the broad message Brosend is sending here? How are we invited to allow the parable to read us?

So what?

- How does your deepened intellectual understanding of these basic facets of storytelling in the life of faith call you to action?
- What will you do differently because you are engaging in this study?

Chapter Two
We Plow the Fields and Scatter: Parables of Growth

Brosend shares a memory from first grade to open this chapter. What is your own experience with growth? Where in your life do you coax growth along? Where do you fight it? With whom do you share growth?

What two problems does Brosend articulate regarding introducing a parable with a claim that it is a story of the kingdom of God? What solution does he suggest?

Brosend invites us to "gather up the evidence from all the parables and sayings about the kingdom and test out our hypotheses of the kingdom on an individual parable after we have come to a tentative conclusion from the entire body of sayings" (p. 19). Revisit his discussion of the individual parables and articulate for yourself the evidence contained therein.

- In what ways do you experience these interpretations as comforting and humbling as Brosend suggests they may be (p. 23)?
- What other interpretations of these stories have you encountered?

Articulate the unique perspectives that Brosend offers in the parables of growth he discusses here (the Mustard Seed, the Seed Growing Automatically, the Unfruitful Fig Tree, the Wheat and the Weeds, and the Sower).

- What "take home" message does he coax from each of these stories?
- Which do you find most persuasive, most compelling?
- Which is your favorite at this moment?
- With which do you struggle?
- Does this feel like good news to you?

Think of some contemporary examples from common life that might express these same concepts. What key facets of the story capture the interpretation?

Having gathered and examined the evidence, what tentative conclusion do you make for the entire body of the parables of growth? To what is God calling you if the kingdom of heaven starts small and spreads everywhere?

- if we are responsible only for sowing and not for growing or even reaping?
- if ours is not to worry about the weeds or another's eternal judgment?
- if profligate evangelism is our charge?

What is this dynamic, this way of life in which we share?

Chapter Three
Seek Ye First: Parables of Seeking

Brosend begins his chapter on seeking by examining two parables of finding. (See pp. 35–39.)

- What conclusions does he come to at the end of this examination?
- What quality of the kingdom of God does Brosend highlight?

In exploring the story of the Lost Sheep, what key lesson from the parable of the Sower does Brosend call forward? (See p. 41.)

- To what are we invited here?
- What challenge does Brosend articulate? What promise will result?

As we continue exploring parables of seeking, on what actions does Brosend focus? What larger pattern of action is highlighted?

- What is the effect of these actions on the individual?
- What is the effect upon the community?

Revisit Brosend's unpacking of the parable of the Prodigal Son on pages 44–51.

- What details do you notice anew in Brosend's examination?
- What is familiar from previous study?

Brosend suggests a pattern of progression and regression in the three stories of seeking (pp. 51–52).

- What pattern does he name?
- How does this match up with your own experience?
- How does this pattern (that the more there is at stake, the less there is the seeker can do about it) sit with you? What do you like about it? What discomforts you?

Brosend cites Thich Nhat Hanh who reminds us that peace is "not just a goal, it is a means to its own fulfillment . . ." (p. 52). Brosend continues with assurance that seeking comes in different guises as evoked by the particular occasion.

- What is your own style when it comes to seeking?
- What experiences shape your willingness to risk?
- Where is God in that?

Chapter Four
When the Roll is Called Up Yonder: Parables of Judgment

In your own words, jot down a definition of "judgment."

Go ahead. Hum the theme from *Dragnet* together. How old were you when this show was broadcast? What did you know about judgment at that age?

In exploring the parable of the Pharisee and the Tax Collector, Brosend offers a historical perspective on the roles of the Pharisee and tax collectors of Jesus' day that defies our Sunday school memories. Revisit those descriptions.

- How does Brosend change our expectations of these characters from "Bible Central Casting"?
- Who asked for what in the prayers?
- What is the surprising juxtaposition that Jesus uses in this parable?

In the parable of the Persistent Widow and the Unjust Judge, the characters are less of a surprise.

- What is it that Brosend labels "the very stuff of faith" (p. 58)?
- How do you feel about judgment when it is in your favor? Is this different than when it is against you?

Revisit Brosend's discussion of the parable of the Rich Man and Lazarus, our first harsh judgment story.
- What two fundamental principles at work in this story does Brosend name?
- How precisely did the rich man fail?
- What is your belief about heaven and hell? How has this belief evolved over time? How does it compare with the world of this story?
- Having heard this parable, how are you feeling about your own life choices? Why?

In Brosend's exploration of the parable of the Unforgiving Servant, the emphasis is on the inability of the first servant to learn from his undeserved forgiveness. Brosend also emphasizes the "absolute necessity of learning from our experience, of learning from God's grace" (p. 63).
- How does one learn to learn from experience? What can facilitate this kind of learning?
- What examples in your own life still haunt or inspire you?

In the parable of the Laborers in the Vineyard, the normal wage is no longer satisfying to the full day workers. Why?
- What do you hope your own response might be in that situation?
- How can you build a life that makes such a response not only possible, but natural?

Brosend next examines three stories about choices and consequences: the parables of the Talents, the Ten Maidens, and the Sheep and the Goats. Revisit his discussion of each.
- What failures lie at the heart of each story?
- What might have helped in each situation?

What will you do differently after thinking about this study?
- What are you going to do with what you know?
- How will you use the grace you have been given (p. 69)?
- What is your job in light of these parables of judgment?
- What is God doing?

Chapter Five
I Have Decided to Follow Jesus: Parables of Decision

Brosend in this chapter shifts attention to the process of deliberation and decision.

- What contrast does Brosend point out in his discussion of the parable of the Two Sons?
- What does Brosend assert is the central decision in this parable? (See p. 73.)
- What exhortation does he give?

In his exploration of stories about planning well to accomplish the task, Brosend comments on the intriguing aspect of this passage: "Jesus treats the life of faith as a matter for deliberate decision and not as a spiritual response to a moment of inspiration" (p. 74). Or, "Can you finish what you start?"

- What is your own history with difficult, almost impossible decisions?
- Do some research on Paul and Luther and Wesley. What can you find about their decision-making processes? How do you imagine it went?
- Are you more like Pascal, wagering on belief, or like Luther, unable to resist God's pursuit? (See pp. 75–76.)
- What calculations did you make before embarking upon a life of faith? How is that working out for you?

Brosend discusses four thoughts that come from reading the story of the Rich Fool. Look at them on pages 76–80.

- What definition do you use of "enough"? How do you show it?
- In what do you think life consists? What has shaped this understanding?
- What in the way you lead your life manifests your beliefs stated above?
- What are you storing up here?

Enjoy the freedom Brosend gives as he invites us into the exploration of the parable of the Dishonest Manager.

- Do we understand our economy today to be a "zero-sum" economy?

- What does that mean? (See p. 82.) How does it affect your reading of the parable?
- Revisit some of the explanations of this parable which Brosend says have failed.
- How comfortable are you with the questions raised and left unanswered about this parable? Are you persuaded?
- What was the result of the decision of the manager?
- What from this story can you apply to your own decision making?

Brosend states that "the parable of the Banquet is about hospitality" (p. 88).

- What light does his discussion of the socio-economic facets of this story shed for you?
- How might you safely and creatively "provide hospitality to those who cannot return the favor" in your own context (p. 88)?
- How does your faith community measure up to the standard of the gospel?

What concepts do you glean from this study to aid and focus your decision-making process individually and corporately? What do you need to support you in this challenge?

Chapter Six
In Christ There Is No East nor West: How to Read a Parable for All You're Worth

Keep in mind Brosend's "limited goals" for this chapter: to tell us everything we need to know about the Good Samaritan, to show us how to use what we have learned from reading parables to develop a method for reading all Scripture, and to change our lives.

- What in your experiences of this study makes you open to these goals?
- Are you still enjoying his wit and clarity?

Brosend offers us extensive comment on the dearth of historical evidence, on Greek linguistics, and on the socio-historical significance of the characters involved in the Good Samaritan parable.

- Which facets of Brosend's discussion of the Good Samaritan are newly engaging to you? Which are familiar?

- How many times in this chapter does Brosend state or imply of the details he shares that "it does not matter"? What does matter?
- How do you get at the "truth at a different level" he discusses around page 101?

In what ways did Jesus go for maximum rhetorical impact in this parable?
- What sharp contrast is elucidated, giving impact to the story? (See p. 95.)
- How do you experience Brosend's question, "But what if we are not the Samaritan?"

Brosend writes of the Good Samaritan, "Because he was willing to stop, he could see what was really going on. . . . And because of the sort of person he was, he had compassion" (p. 97).
- What other examples can you think of from Scripture that commend such stopping?
- How is this parable unique?

Brosend and other New Testament scholars include the story of Mary and Martha in the context for reading the parable of the Good Samaritan (p. 98).
- What impact does this have on the interpretation of the parable?
- Where does the balance lie in your own life between discipleship and ministry? Where is the balance in the life of your community?
- How do you know where that balance belongs?

Have you understood Brosend's explanation of *hermeneutic*? What other explanations can you research and share? (Hey! www.wiki pedia.com is not half bad here . . .)

What two juxtapositions does Brosend name as "key to understanding the meaning of the narrative" (p. 102)? Together, what do these juxtapositions reveal?

Brosend reveals one of his "foundational principles for interpreting Scripture: the Bible is the Word of God because it speaks God's truth to all people for all time, not because it can be demonstrated to be historically accurate to a given time and place." He celebrates the very openness to more than one interpretation as parables' ways of teaching us that "Jesus *liked* polyvalency . . . thrived on it" (p. 102).

- If this is indeed the case, how do we as individuals and communities of faith discern the authentic voice of God in the Scripture? How do we know which message is ours to claim?
- Revisit what Brosend has to say on the suppleness required to read parables, on the lightness of reading they demand. What is the invitation parables issue? (See p. 103.)

On page 103, Brosend writes, "The *hermeneutical* issue is to determine the basis on which you decide to read one command literally and binding across all time, and another as not. I said it was important." He goes on to name as a false choice and something from which we are freed, the "rote literalism that privileges one reading to the exclusion of all others and makes our approach to Scripture a perpetual choice between right and wrong" (p. 103).

- What guidance does Brosend offer to help us avoid losing the meaning of the text?
- What assumptions does this approach make?

Brosend closes his study with a statement of things that matter in ministry.

- List the five things that he names. (See pp. 106–8.)
- Review his discussion of how he reached this conclusion and how it impacts his decisions in ministry. Would you alter his list to make it your own? How?
- What primary tasks does Brosend call us to based in his understanding of the gospel in parables? What effects are anticipated?

Did Bill Brosend succeed in the third of his goals for this chapter? How are you different for having engaged in this study together? How do you claim the gospel's unique message for you and live into the kingdom of God anew?

The Rev. Helen McPeak lives in Las Vegas, Nevada, where the strangeness of life often arrests her. Parish priest, marriage partner, and parent of two boys, her mind is frequently left in doubt sufficient to tease it into active thought.

NOTES

Introduction to the Series

1. 332.
2. "The Anglican Church has always existed in a context of rival ways of ordering the Church. On the one hand it has refused an authoritarian solution, where one central authority holds out the attractive possibility of getting rid of the messiness of debate, dissent, and rival interpretations of scripture by pronouncements and commands that permit no argument. On the other hand, it has resisted the sort of diversity in which everyone is free to do according to their own interpretation and conscience, and no one is ultimately accountable to anyone else" (Ford, 367).

Introduction

1. Fred B. Craddock, *As One without Authority* (reissue; Atlanta: Chalice Press, 2001). Also, *Overhearing the Gospel* (revised and expanded edition; Atlanta: Chalice Press, 2001). You can enjoy some of Dr. Craddock's own sermons in *Cherry Log Sermons* (Louisville: Westminster John Knox Press, 2001).

Chapter One:
I Love to Tell the Story: Jesus the Storyteller

1. Quoted in C. H. Dodd, *The Parables of the Kingdom* (New York: Charles Scribner's Sons, 1961), 1–2.
2. Adolf Jülicher, *Die Gleichnisreden Jesu*, 2 vols. (Tübingen: J. C. B. Mohr, 1910). The work has never been translated.
3. Joachim Jeremias, *The Parables of Jesus*, 2nd rev. ed., trans. S.H. Hooke (New York: Charles Scribner's Sons, 1972).
4. Kenneth Bailey, *Poet and Peasant* and *Through Peasant Eyes*, combined ed. (Grand Rapids: Eerdmans, 1980).

5. Of particular importance for my own work is my teacher John R. Don-ahue, *The Gospel in Parables* (Philadelphia: Fortress Press, 1988) and John Dominic Crossan, *In Parables* (New York: Harper and Row, 1973).

6. Vernon K. Robbins, *Exploring the Textures of Texts* (Valley Forge, PA: Trinity Press International, 1996), 7.

7. Ibid., 40.

8. Ibid., 95.

9. Ibid., 120.

10. Dodd, *Parables of the Kingdom*, 5.

11. Ibid.

Chapter Two:
We Plow the Fields and Scatter: Parables of Growth

1. Aristotle's *Art of Rhetoric*, Loeb Classical Library (Cambridge: Cambridge University Press, 1926) and Quintilian's *Institutio Oratoria*, 4 vols., Loeb Classical Library (Cambridge: Cambridge University Press, 1920) are the best known examples.

2. Those remembering their literature class will recognize the "tenor" (date) and "vehicle" (octopus).

3. The *Gospel of Thomas* is an important supplemental witness to the Jesus Tradition known from various fragments prior to its discovery in the Egyptian desert along with other Nag Hamadi Codices. Because its date of composition is widely contested, and its provenance unknown, we will not consider the parable versions found in Thomas. The interested reader may consult one of the books listed in "Continuing the Conversation" for more information. Scott, for one, consistently makes reference to Thomas.

4. I assume "Markan Priority" throughout this study, along with the vast majority of New Testament scholars. That is, the Gospel of Mark was written first, around 70 CE, and Matthew and Luke, written fifteen or so years later, used Mark for the outline, or synopsis (hence Synoptic Gospels), along with another common source conventionally designated "Q" (from the German *Quelle*, "saying"), and material unique to each.

5. Kilaim 3.2. Herbert Danby, *The Mishnah* (Oxford: Oxford University Press, 1933), 32.

6. If you ever wondered at Thanksgiving Eucharist where Henry Alford came up with the line in "Come, Ye Thankful People, Come"—"First the grain, then the ear, then the full grain shall appear"—now you know.

7. Parable scholars are divided about the "authenticity" of the interpretations, that is, whether Jesus, the early Church, or the Evangelist is best

understood as the "author" of the interpretations, a question beyond the concerns of this study but which can be explored in any of the fine books listed in the Further Reading section. As noted in the first chapter, this issue was a particular concern of Joachim Jeremias.

8. William Brosend, *The Recovery of Allegory* (Unpublished dissertation, 1993).

9. Mary Ann Tolbert, *Sowing the Gospel* (Minneapolis: Fortress Press, 1989).

10. I am well aware that Mark 4:13 says "parable" not "story"—"Do you not understand this parable? Then how will you understand all the parables?" However, the Greek word *parabolē*, like the Hebrew word *mashal*, cannot in its biblical use be limited to a single rhetorical form, and to find our way through the parable vs. allegory thickets it is helpful to use the neutral term "story."

11. Ibid.

Chapter Three:
Seek Ye First: Parables of Seeking

1. "Finding Is the First Act," *The Complete Poems of Emily Dickinson* (New York: Little, Brown, and Company, 1961), 414.

2. Pliny, *Natural History*, 3 vols., Loeb Classical Library, trans. H. Rackham (Cambridge, MA: Harvard University Press, 1971), Book 37.

3. Later in the tradition, in a song now found in the apocryphal *Acts of Thomas*, a "Hymn to the Pearl," wisdom tradition and the gnostic redeemer myth mix in the story of a prince sent from heaven to retrieve a "pearl."

4. Thich Nhat Hanh, *Peace Is Every Step* (New York: Bantam Books, 1991).

Chapter Four:
When the Roll Is Called Up Yonder: Parables of Judgment

1. Berakoth 28 b cited by Joachim Jeremias, *The Parables of Jesus*, 142.

Chapter Five:
I Have Decided to Follow Jesus: Parables of Decision

1. Dietrich Bonhoeffer, *The Cost of Discipleship*, trans. R. H. Fuller (New York: MacMillan, 1963), 45–60.

2. Ibid., 89.

3. Dodd, *Parables of the Kingdom*, 17.

4. Dan Otto Via Jr., *The Parables* (Philadelphia: Fortress Press, 1967), 155–62.

Chapter Six:
In Christ There Is No East nor West:
How to Read a Parable for All You're Worth

1. Anthony deMello, *The Song of the Bird* (New York: Image Books, 1984), 82–83.
2. E. Allison Peers, trans., *The Life of Teresa of Jesus: The Autobiography of Teresa of Avila* (New York: Image Books, 1960), 124–33.
3. See my article, "What Matters in Ministry," in the Alban Institute journal *Congregations* (Spring 2004).

SUGGESTIONS
FOR FURTHER READINGS

My friend Tom Long likes to say that he can determine in five minutes when a clergy person "died" intellectually by looking at their library. If there is not more than a book or two published after the date on her or his seminary diploma, they are as good as dead. You might think this true about the books on the parables mentioned below, because most of them come from at least fifteen years ago. In this case, however, it is a reflection of a now passed high point in parable interpretation. Simply put, there has not been that much written about the parables since 1990 or so.

Throughout this study I have mentioned the work of C. H. Dodd, *The Parables of the Kingdom* (New York: Charles Scribner's Sons, 1961) and Joachim Jeremias, *The Parables of Jesus*, 2nd rev. ed., trans. S.H. Hooke (New York: Charles Scribner's Sons, 1972), and for good reason—every interpreter who came after them built on the foundation they so carefully laid. If you like to see how things develop over time, you may want to read one or the other.

Of the other authors mentioned from time to time, I especially commend the parables book of my teacher, John R. Donahue, S.J., *The Gospel in Parables* (Philadelphia: Fortress Press, 1988) and the fine work of Bernard Brandon Scott, *Hear Then the Parable* (Minneapolis: Fortress Press, 1989). Professor Donahue attends faithfully to the context of the synoptic parables in ways I did only sporadically in this conversation, while Professor Scott attempts to determine the "originating parable" that, in his view, was often altered by the tradition before being recorded in the gospels, which explains his frequent reference to versions found in the *Gospel of Thomas*.

Among the more recent parable studies three should be mentioned. While originally published in the 1980s, Robert Farrar Capon's fine work has now been gathered into a single volume, *Kingdom, Grace, Judgment: Paradox, Outrage, and Vindication in the Parables of Jesus* (Grand Rapids, MI: Eerdmans, 2002), and offers many excellent expositions. The introductory material and appendices in Charles Hedrick's *Parables as Poetic Fictions* (Peabody, MA: Hendrickson Publishers, 1994) is excellent, as are his readings of the six parables he examines in detail. From a more traditionalist perspective, Arland Hultgren's *The Parables of Jesus, a Commentary* (Grand Rapids, MI: Eerdmans, 2000) is well worth reading.

ABOUT THE AUTHOR

William Brosend is an Episcopal priest in the Diocese of Kentucky, and Associate Professor of Homiletics at the School of Theology of the University of the South in Sewanee, Tennessee. Previously he served for five years as Associate Director of the Louisville Institute, a grant-making and convening program of the Religion Division of the Lilly Endowment, Inc. Bill studied at Denison University (B.A.), and the Divinity Schools of Vanderbilt University (M.Div.) and the University of Chicago (Ph.D.). In addition to numerous articles, essays, and curriculum, he is the author of a commentary, *James and Jude* (New Cambridge Bible Commentary, Cambridge University Press, 2004) and a contributor to two volumes in the *New Proclamation Lectionary Commentary* series (Fortress Press, 2005, 2007). His next project, *Jesus and the Rhetoric of Proclamation*, will explore the implications of the rhetoric of Jesus in the Synoptic Gospels for how we preach about Jesus.

The son and grandson of Baptist clergy, Bill was himself ordained and served four parishes in the American Baptist Churches, and taught at three Baptist seminaries. In 2000 he and his wife, Christine, followed their hearts out of Baptist life, beginning a journey to the Episcopal Church that culminated in their confirmation (2002) and Bill's ordination to the priesthood (2005). Bill, Christine (an accomplished church musician, soprano soloist, and teacher), and Emily, their daughter (a singer like her mother and a writer like her father—no one knows where the dancing comes from), live in Sewanee.